To
the millions
of teachers in our Republic,
this volume is dedicated
with tender appreciation
and honorable humility.
Also in recognition
of our failure
to sing their praises
as they deserve.

Morris L. Ernst is author of:

UTOPIA, 1976
TOUCH WOOD
SO FAR SO GOOD
THE BEST IS YET
UNTITLED: THE DIARY OF MY 72D YEAR
THE FIRST FREEDOM
TOO BIG
THE ULTIMATE POWER
AMERICA'S PRIMER

And co-author of:

THE COMPARATIVE INTERNATIONAL GAZETTEER
CENSORSHIP: THE SEARCH FOR THE OBSCENE
PRIVACY: THE RIGHT TO BE LET ALONE
HOLD YOUR TONGUE
TO THE PURE
FOR BETTER OR WORSE
REPORT ON THE AMERICAN COMMUNIST
THE PEOPLE KNOW BEST
AMERICAN SEXUAL BEHAVIOR AND THE KINSEY REPORT

The
Teacher

Edited
by
MORRIS L. ERNST

PRENTICE-HALL, INC.   *Englewood Cliffs, N.J.*

The Teacher, edited by Morris L. Ernst

© 1967 by Joan E. Goldstein

Library of Congress Catalog Card Number: 67–23505

Printed in the United States of America

T88806

Prentice-Hall International, Inc., *London*
Prentice-Hall of Australia, Pty. Ltd., *Sydney*
Prentice-Hall of Canada, Ltd., *Toronto*
Prentice-Hall of India Private Ltd., *New Delhi*
Prentice-Hall of Japan, Inc., *Tokyo*

The Teacher

CONTENTS

☀

FOREWORD

This book grew out of a sort of intellectual parlor game which was itself a reflection both of the vital role that good teaching plays in our lives and of the neglect that the good teachers all too often have to endure. Our society has paid much lip service to education but has often downgraded the educator. Therefore, it was fun to fling into the talk of almost any group of people, as my wife Margaret and I did with friends in our home, the challenging question:

"Did you ever have a teacher to whom you will die in debt?"

Almost invariably the reply was an outpouring of genuine gratitude to the ones who had first excited their minds, taught them good work habits, opened up new avenues to intellectual adventure, gave them personal assurance, or in some other way proved to be a turning point in their lives.

From the sum of all these influences and from the

way the stories were told—often the teller had never thought of the debt before—it began to appear that a collection of these experiences might illuminate some valuable facets of the teaching process. Also that it might enhance the prestige of genuine excellence in teaching. So we began to ask the story-tellers for written vignettes of the actual experience, whether it was in kindergarten or graduate school or anywhere in between. As the idea of embodying them in a book took form, members of the staff of the National Education Association helped by providing wise counsel and enlisting some of the contributors.

The aim has been to capture in print some of the quiet excitement that occurs when a teacher does "it" to a pupil. As might be expected, this may have been remote from the bald facts of the actual subject matter for that particular class or course. A teacher of French, biology or algebra may have added to the pupil's stockpile of knowledge, but this gift was minimal compared to that difficult-to-isolate stroke of intellectual lightning which so often changed an entire path of life for an unsuspecting student.

One of the revealing features of these stories is that the lightning never seems to strike in quite the same way twice. Each of the experiences here chronicled was unique, governed by the individual characteristics of the teacher and pupil involved. The teachers may have been stern or lenient, aloof or intimate, eccentric or conventional, vastly knowledgeable or relatively uninformed. The pupils may have been eager or reluctant, industrious or lazy, slow or quick, docile or rebellious. But however the ingredients of personalities were mixed, somehow the flash was generated, the flash of a clear and meaningful communication between two minds.

This volume could have been expanded to thousands of examples of personal wonder teachers. But the editor preferred to solicit stories from a wide variety of men and women who might be articulate in declaring their thanks to *the* teacher. So the book represents a cross section of people in various trades and professions, including some who carry on the mighty occupation of homemaker, even if part-time. Their one common denominator except for appreciation of a teacher is a gift for expressing themselves.

Many of the contributors, after digging out of the storehouse of memory their reasons for gratitude, would say:

"If she is still alive, I'll look her up tomorrow because I never truly told her what she did to and for me."

Others wanted to write about a parent or a divine. Some who were of tender years, say under 25, were inclined to ask:

"Can I name a book instead of a teacher?"

Such a response only indicated that perspective is often needed to reach the richness of recognition of that gift-bearing teacher. Nevertheless, few, even among school dropouts, have not enjoyed at least one truly significant relationship in the setting of formal education. To some fortunate ones, the experience has been vouchsafed with more than one teacher.

Former Vice President Henry A. Wallace was a good example of the general reaction to our approach. When I asked him if he had memories of some teacher to whom he would die in debt, he wrote:

"My two best teachers were my mother and George Washington Carver. In 1894 Carver was studying for a Master's degree in botany at Iowa State College at Ames and was a good friend of my father, who was professor of dairying there. Carver took me on botanizing expeditions and taught me to recognize the parts of a flower, to distinguish species, and many other things. A little later, my mother showed me how to hybridize flowers."

Carver, of course, was the great agricultural chemist who later taught and worked some of his wonders of research at Tuskegee Institute. Wallace himself may have done more for man through his work with hybrid corn, which vastly increased the world's food supply, than by his political career. But neither Carver nor Mrs. Wallace were among his formal teachers, about whom I wanted to know, and he added:

"I remember most vividly 'Bugs' Summers, professor of zoology at Iowa State, my first formal teacher. (I don't remember his initials or first name.) He made 'Evolution' seem exciting and dynamic to me. He was on fire with his feeling concerning it and he imparted that feeling to others. He hammered into us the meaning of the phrase, 'Ontogeny recapitulates phylogeny.' The scientific base for the unity of life began to appear."

Unfortunately Henry Wallace did not live to expand on this theme of the awakening of his scientific interests and just how "Bugs" Summers transferred the fire of his zeal to his promising pupils.

In my own case, I hold a fond but very faint recollection of one teacher in high school. I cannot say, however, that this left much of a mark on me, certainly not one I can discern myself. My only significant teacher came along early in college, in 1905. He was Ted Lewis, who was on the faculty of Williams, a small college in the beautiful Berkshire Hills, to which I had gone from high school in New York, influenced by no special educational fervor but simply because a couple of my classmates had enrolled there and I had flunked the entrance exams to Harvard. Lewis made his impact upon me through what must now seem a most improbable medium. He expounded and explained to me the political philosophy of David Lloyd George and the application of that philosophy to the functions and scope of government.

Ted was the son of a Welsh coal miner, an immigrant to our shores, and he had attained two of the great goals of the American dream—a college education and some fame as a pitcher for one of Boston's major league baseball teams. To me he represented the Horatio Alger legend of rags to riches in the very best sense of the word "riches." My own sports were tennis and bowling, so I had a very real envy of the athlete who performed publicly in the arenas of our more highly competitive team contests. I was also rather lonely, envying the more sophisticated students at Williams, although I remember my college days as generally quite happy. So I listened to Ted's words with acute and magnified attention, both in the classroom and across the table in his modest kitchen, to which he sometimes invited me.

The most memorable of those words were his worshipful discourses on Lloyd George, the Welsh "radical" who talked about taking care of the aged, succoring the maimed and providing medical aid to the ill, not as a charity bestowed by the more fortunate members of society, but as the simple duty of the State. This disturbing if not actually revolutionary posture of the future British Prime Minister intrigued me in 1905. It matters not that my mind-opening professor never in his own life went beyond the Bismarck–Lloyd George political concepts.

Tall and lean, preserving the appearance of an athlete in training, he was a handsome man whose maturity impressed me at the time although I suppose he was only about ten years my senior. He was popular enough as a teacher, but I do not recall that very many if any other Williams students reacted to his philosophy as I did.

Until Ted broadened my outlook, I never had thought of government as more than a device to get the streets cleaned, operate the courts, employ the police and provide an army and navy. "Public welfare" were empty words in our Constitution as I had been taught them. But by 1932 I was able to relate Ted's talk about Lloyd George to the social revolution designed by Franklin D. Roosevelt after the Hoover depression. Lewis had given me my first concept of the relation in law between the sovereign and the people. Carrying me beyond the notion that government existed merely to supply prosaic services, he opened to me the role of government in my life, the importance of welfare legislation to insure progress in society, and the place that law and lawyers must play.

I am not sure if I ever conveyed my thanks to him. So now, as I look back, I feel particular pleasure in recording here that I shall die in debt to Ted Lewis. Of course he himself was dead before I fully realized the fact. But as this book took shape, I found that my experience was not unusual. In these reports, I have been struck by the frequency with which the writers express regret that they never thanked their teachers.

Striking also was the aptness of the etymology of the words contributors used in telling about their educational highlights. My favorite is that "school" in the Greek meant "to spare time" or "leisure" or even originally "a resting" or "pausing." Often that was more applicable than anything associated with the word "work" to the adventure of the mind which the contributor was describing.

It also is significant that "teacher" derives from "to show" while "student" means "to be eager about"—and those two phrases are a capsule summary of what most of the stories in this book are about. "Instructor" came from "to build in," which is also close to many of these accounts, while "professor" represents a variation in the sense of its Latin derivation, "to manifest, confess or avow."

In the sense these words are used, there may seem to be no good reason to omit the contribution which a parent, relative, friend, minister or even a book may have made to the enlightenment of an individual. But there is a very special enrichment that flows in unique fashion from a trained and dedicated teacher to a pupil who is endowed with curiosity. It was this speciality, exclusively practiced within a professional group which is not always fully appreciated in our society, that we have wished to describe here. The descriptions of it in the pages that follow are, I think, the best possible explanation of how it works and what it can accomplish.

We Americans are among the fortunate peoples of the earth who have any opportunity to experience this great adventure. After all, one billion, or more than half of the men and women over the age of 14 in the more than 220 nations of our planet, are totally illiterate. Not only can they not learn from the written word, but they are completely teacherless in the sense that they never will be exposed to the possibility of that spark which passes from one person specially trained to communicate it to another.

When we, as a nation, fully appreciate this fact of our own good fortune, then at long last we will vote the money which schools and teachers deserve. Surely the lead in this should be taken by those of us who are grateful to our teachers or to some one of them, to those men and women who seemed unreasonably old to us at the time, who gave us sound work habits or excited our own intellectual faculties, who often changed the entire course of our lives.

MORRIS L. ERNST

*

"YOU WILL WIND UP IN SING SING"

Edward S. Silver

❋❋❋❋❋❋❋❋❋❋❋❋❋❋❋❋❋❋❋❋❋❋❋❋❋❋❋❋❋❋❋❋

Admitted to the bar in 1925, Edward S. Silver spent the next four years as an Assistant United States Attorney in New York, then rose to eminence in private practice. District Attorney of Kings County (Brooklyn) from 1954 to 1965, he was president of both State and national prosecutor associations. He is now Surrogate of Kings County.

❋❋❋❋❋❋❋❋❋❋❋❋❋❋❋❋❋❋❋❋❋❋❋❋❋❋❋❋❋❋❋❋

※

"YOU WILL
WIND UP IN
SING SING"

Edward S. Silver

As I think back, we had no grounds for calling her "Old Lady" Danford. It may be that now, reaching for 65, I've developed greater care and possibly some sensitiveness in the use of the word "old."

Miss Danford was my teacher in the first half of the sixth grade—6A we called it—in P.S. 164 in Brooklyn. That was over half a century ago. As I think back, and for good reason, I have a pretty clear picture of Miss Danford. She could not have been over thirty years old. She was a good-looking gal, too.

If she were a man, she would have been a drill sergeant in the Marines. She took no guff from anybody, and if the occasion called for it she was fast and good with her hands.

I think that Miss Danford had a unique way of getting under your skin. I wouldn't call it inspiration—except perhaps inspiration in reverse. "You *could* amount to something but you never will," was one song of her repertoire.

Akin to being a traitor to your country was a violation of her rule of "absolutely no talking on a fire drill." I was a gabby kid and the monitor, Itchky Moel, reported me violating her no-talking rule at almost every fire drill. I was not the only violator on the occasion I have in mind. There were four of us. Green—we called him Greeny—and two other kids and myself. She told two of us to take our seats. "You'll get a chance to learn the rules next term. You will be left back."

She wasn't kidding. She never did. She stood up to Greeny. Before he had a chance to know what happened, she had clipped him one-two, one-two, with a right back-hand-palm, back-hand-palm. She came up to me. I was forewarned. Up came her fast right and up came my elbows just a bit faster. She hit my right elbow. A bit flushed and lips tightened she staccatoed: "Keep your hands down."

"Yes, Ma'am," I replied quickly.

I made up my mind to do just that. I wanted no complications with a possible note to my Mom. I'd rather take her whacks than Mom's look of despair and her "What'll be with you? What'll be with you?"

Up came her hand and again up came my elbows a bit faster than her hands. Her eyes narrowed, she bit her lip.

"Go out to the hall and stay there."

I went, upbraiding myself for what I had done. I didn't know what was to happen now.

She came out and drilled me with her eyes for some seconds and then pronounced my fate with clipped, clear words: "You *could* amount to something but you never will—you, Silver, will wind up in Sing Sing."

I saw her hand coming and my elbows automatically came up again. But she fooled me. She grabbed my hair and pulled. I felt as if I were being scalped. I have a pretty good crop of hair even now, but in those days I had a *real* crop. I used to get a haircut twice a year, every Passover and Tabernacles, whether I needed it or not. I was a sucker for her new attack—no defense at all.

Miss Danford never let any infraction go by without some prompt action. She dispensed a rough justice, if you want to call it that. Everybody agrees that kids are pretty diabolical in the stunts they can dream up to harass a teacher. A wooden matchstick rolled underfoot makes quite a rumbling noise. You could roll the matchstick while you were reciting and complain at the same time to the teacher about being disturbed by the noise. If Miss Danford asked you, "Are you making that noise?" you could deny it while still rumbling the match.

The rumbling match came into being because there was no besting Miss Danford. She was smart, she was quick and not much time went by between getting caught and getting punished. Now we had her baffled.

One midmorning during "reading" the rumbling match was heard. Miss Danford said nothing. She picked up her red Barnes' history book off the desk and went to the back of the room. (That Barnes' history was not a history so far as we kids were concerned. It was a club in the shape of a book.)

"Keep your eyes front."

She walked up an aisle slowly. No one moved.

Wham! Slotkin got a shot with the Barnes. Wham! Greeny got a shot next. She went to the back of the room again. Whack! I got it this time. Moe Alderman got it next. Perlstein got it last. She ordered the five of us to the front of the room.

"There is just a chance *one* of you is not involved with the rumbling. If it's so, I'm sorry. There is to be no rumbling of matches."

The injunction came slowly and clearly. It sounded as if to violate it meant clear and positive extinction. (How did she know about the matches?) She seemed to look directly at me. I guess all of us felt the same way. We were all involved. The only mistake was that she missed two of the conspirators.

"You *could* amount to something but you never will. I *thought* you'd wind up in Sing Sing, now I *know* you will. Get to your seats."

She put Barnes on the desk and went on with "reading" as if nothing had happened. No wooden match ever rumbled again in Miss Danford's class.

I never got a straight "good word" from Miss Danford. This is what I mean. One morning Mr. Preston, the principal of 164, walked in and, as was his wont, queried the class on our work. He was particularly interested in arithmetic. He'd ask a question and ask for volunteers to raise their hands for the answers. I raised my hand again and again and was called on for several answers which happened to be correct. After Mr. Preston left, Miss Danford turned to Slotkin and me:

"You *could* amount to something." This time she didn't say, "but you won't," although with her emphasis on "could" I thought she might just as well have said it.

But the fact remained that she didn't. "You could amount to something" began to sound good to me. I repeated in my mind what Miss Danford had said to me, "You could amount to something." I sure wanted to believe it. Gradually "but you won't" faded away, and I accepted her statement: "You could amount to something." I did my best not to cross her again. Coming from Miss Danford a little praise went a long way.

I have the feeling now as I look back that "Old Lady" Danford had a way of her own to make you do what she thought you could. "Silver, you will wind up in Sing Sing." You know, I did in a way, but on the right side of the wall.

※

THE MELODY
LINGERS ON

Fannie Hurst

✳

THE MELODY
LINGERS ON

Fannie Hurst

In the restless coming-aware years of my high school life in St. Louis, Missouri, a slight, goateed man stands out against a background of faceless silhouettes almost dimmed by time.

His name was William Schuyler, descendant of a Dutch-American family of long lineage. Even though he is long since gone, I owe this man a debt which, alas, I never acknowledged. Realization of it came tardily, and when it did it was too late.

In fantasy I can see myself running down the corridor of time that leads to his grave, calling: "Mr. Schuyler, wait a moment, I have something to tell you."

But during the years he was assistant-principal in Central High School I had much to tell him, things that as an only child and a lone-wolf by temperament, I had never before been able to express.

I was frequently sent "up to the office," in high school parlance, for a long line of minor classroom misdemeanors, such as prompting, reading extraneous books during study hours, ignoring classroom rulings, writing essays for pupils in exchange for geometry homework.

To my pleasurable surprise Mr. Schuyler seemed little interested in these various violations, the disciplines inherent in pedagogy seeming to concern him only secondarily. His interest, straight as a crow flies, was in the psychology of the child, the wherefore, the whyfore.

I realize now that through gentle processes of drawing me out, he diagnosed and articulated for me much of the groping confusion that must have been responsible for my itchy malaise.

In a way Mr. Schuyler, up in his high intellectual echelon, and I down in my lowly one, shared dilemmas. He was lonely and miscast. I also gropingly understood that for a man who must be in his sixties, which to me at the time was the last lap of the life-span, he had not gone far. Yet he seemed so infinitely the superior of the principal and most members of the faculty.

In my case he managed to siphon from my mind much that I had never articulated even to myself. He drew me out, queried at length my dishonest device of writing compositions for classmates, probed and asked questions that gave me the opportunity to air my ego and my major interest, namely, writing.

He was critical of my promiscuous extracurricular reading matter and gave me lists of books I might have ignored in my haphazard browsings in the St. Louis public libraries. He read the "literary efforts" I produced in his office as disciplinary measures and encouraged me to follow my inclination to write. I was not to know until after I graduated that Mr. Schuyler was himself the author of several books, collections of essays and belles lettres.

In our semisouthern city Mr. Schuyler enjoyed the advantages and suffered the disadvantages of being ahead of his time. The winds before the dawn must have been carrying to him intimations of things to come. He asked me one day what I thought about our school of 1,400 white pupils. Where were the colored children who formed so large a population in our town?

I had never thought about it, nor noticed their conspicuous absence. We had Negro ghettos, an invisible wall separating them from the white majority. Our colored people served as janitors, did our housework, washed and ironed, tended babies, worked on the levees loading and unloading Mississippi River boats, collected garbage. If household domestics fell ill, we carried a pot of boiled ham and greens down to their shanties or tenements, supplied coal for their poorly heated rooms, and that was that.

The word "Mammy" was still in affectionate family circulation. A neighbor of ours was so fond of her housemaid, Cassie, that she stipulated Cassie should be buried at her feet. My Mississippi-born father, who was later to see the light, remarked when I first opened the subject with him that Negroes were all right in their place. It was that simple in my pre-W. S. (William Schuyler) era.

I owed him many social and cultural awakenings

which I did not realize at the time, any more than I did the glaring flaw, under my very eyes, in our democratic system.

Likewise he repossessed, revised, indeed fumigated my reading habits, diverting me from haphazard pickings off library shelves and the limitations of prescribed classroom curriculum.

I thought a great deal about Mr. Schuyler during high school years, continuing to devise misdemeanors that would send me "up to the office." Mr. Schuyler died after I finished high school and had entered college. I asked many local people about him. They did not know him.

I did!

✳

HE
LIKED
STUDENTS

John Fischer

※

HE
LIKED
STUDENTS

John Fischer

By contemporary standards, the late Dr. Cortes A. M.
Ewing would be considered far from a model professor.
He did not skip rapidly from one university to another
in pursuit of higher pay and status; most of his adult life
he spent—quite happily, I think—at a nonprestigious
school, the University of Oklahoma. He never schemed
to become a college president, or even a dean. He
shunned the outside consulting jobs and government
assignments which offer the traditional academic route
to money and fame. Although he did more than his
share of research and publication, he never thought of
such work as an irksome obligation. He saw it as part of
the job of a good teacher. His only discernible ambition
was shockingly unfashionable: he liked to teach.

Odder yet, he liked students. Some recent graduates,
who have gone all through college without ever speaking to a professor outside the classroom, may find this
hard to believe—but Ewing spent nearly all of his spare

time with undergraduates. As Dr. John G. Kemeny, chairman of the Dartmouth mathematics department, recently pointed out, such behavior is almost unheard-of today; even graduate students are lucky to get a few informal words with a professor, and professors frequently consider undergraduates as far beneath notice as campus squirrels. Ewing thought they were the most important people in the university.

He was the first teacher who ever asked me to his home. Since he was married to the prettiest member of the faculty, and I was at least as gawky and shy as the average freshman, I arrived stuttering with mixed eagerness and apprehension. But within fifteen minutes he and Ina had somehow made me feel entirely at home. Before the evening was over I was talking more freely than I ever had to anyone—not just about government and politics, which I studied under him, but about my own ambitions and schemes for remaking the world. If most of this was nonsense, as I now suspect, he gave no hint of boredom. Instead he listened with enthusiasm, throwing in a few words now and then of comment, encouragement and subtly disguised guidance.

During the next four years I spent a lot of time around the Ewing household—even dropping in uninvited for a meal now and then when I was entirely out of money. Lots of other students did the same, and the long evenings often turned into unpremeditated (by us, at least) seminars. By common consent, Ewing was the best lecturer on the campus; but he also was one of the most provocative, and often a furious argument which had started during the final twenty minutes of his class would continue for hours in his living room that evening.

Without our quite realizing it, certain ideas began to seep into our minds—maybe into our bones. For example, the notion that politics is an exciting and important business, not only for politicians but for everybody. The startling idea that one man—no matter how young, obscure and poor—could make things happen in the corridors of government if he applied his little leverage at the right time and place. The idea that the art of government is the highest and most difficult of the arts, and the necessary foundation for all other arts and for civilization itself. The idea that politics is not necessarily a dirty business, but that it can be the noblest (and sometimes the most heartbreaking) of callings.

With the unconscious selfishness of young people, most of us probably never got around to telling Ewing that he had opened invaluable doors for us. But I think he knew it, because scores of his students went on to responsible roles in public life—and many kept a steady correspondence with him as long as he lived. One of them, who used to infest Ewing's house at the same time I did, was Carl Albert, now Majority Leader of the House of Representatives. Another was Dean Wooldridge, a brilliant scientist who became cofounder and president of a major electronics firm, but still keeps a lively interest in public affairs. Others are Washington lawyers, editorial writers and foreign correspondents, civil servants and active politicians—from the courthouse level to the top echelons of federal power. Some of us are now engaged in raising money to endow a

Cortes A. M. Ewing Lectureship at the University of Oklahoma. It will be an inadequate memorial, but we don't know how to accomplish what we would really like to do in his name: convince professors and university administrators everywhere that the prime job of a teacher is to teach . . . that no amount of research and learned monographs can take the place of teaching . . . that the best teaching (as Socrates demonstrated) doesn't happen in the lecture hall, but in uncounted hours of informal, intensely personal conversation with students . . . and that a faculty member who does not enjoy the company of students, however callow, demanding and exasperating, probably is in the wrong profession.

✳

CONCOMITANCE, J. SALWYN SCHAPIRO AND ME

Gerel Rubien

※※*※*※*※*※*※*※*※*※*※*※*※*※*※*※*

Gerel Rubien, former President of the Women's Trade Union League, which played a unique and significant role in the American labor movement, is now educational director of the Undergarment and Negligee Workers Union, I.L.G.W.U. Besides her work with 15,000 women members, she lectures on labor history and economics and is active in political education and community efforts for liberal laws.

※※*※*※*※*※*※*※*※*※*※*※*※*※*※*※*

＊

CONCOMITANCE,
J. SALWYN SCHAPIRO
AND ME

Gerel Rubien

Something was happening in the pink part of the map at the same time events occurred in the green part of the map. And these separated events had relevancy to each other.

That was the astonishing revelation for which Professor J. Salwyn Schapiro was responsible. It was a broad wedge of light cast, for me, on history, and an entirely new way of looking at world events, past and present.

This staggering historical concept came to me by accident. During my last year at Columbia University's School of Journalism I had a run-in with the Dean. It wasn't the first. He was a fearsome gentleman, very British, very authoritative. This seemed natural, for in my undergraduate days, between World Wars I and II, teachers were authoritative persons to be impersonally respected. It never occurred to me that they might have private lives. I suppose I thought they disappeared into the cupboard, along with the chalk and erasers, at the end of the school day.

I was bright; my marks had always been good. Since I had had an unusual childhood I was, or thought I was, more sophisticated than the general run of undergraduates. I had started to read when I was a little more than four, and so had a good memory, as children who have taught themselves to read before they could spell often do. In elementary school I was teachers' favorite. I enjoyed my lessons and was selected for school demonstrations, especially when it came to learning poetry by heart.

Maybe by the time I came to college I was brash. I knew *everything!* But I was respectful of my instructors. I was respectful of the Dean and impressed by his English accent. "Shedule" I took in stride as well as "la*bor*atry," and I went around the campus for days muttering, "One looks it up in the ency*clop*ida." I laughed dutifully at his academic jokes—at least I smiled the first few times as he locked the classroom door against latecomers to his course and uttered his standard witticism, "Now we are all on the right side, as the bridegroom said to the bride."

I couldn't ascribe his obvious disapproval of me to anything so human as sheer human dislike. How could he dislike me? Professors were not supposed to have such mundane reactions, anyway, in spite of the elderly instructor (he must have been in his early forties) who, during an interview in his office, made some obvious references to the lighter side of male-female relationships and put his arm around me. It was such a shock that I thought I had imagined what would now be called a "pass."

One day, on a consultation on some academic matter during which I was voluble, the Dean inquired in his frigidly acid manner whether my mother spoke English at home. My mother! She had spent years trying to eliminate the unnecessary "got" from "Have you got?" and her oft-repeated injunction was that an abundant use of either slang or profanity in conversation indicated a paucity of vocabulary.

I left the Dean's office in stunned silence, imagining the explosion that would have occurred had I repeated his question to my Edwardian, precisely-spoken mother.

One spring morning, a few weeks before graduation, I was summoned into the Awful Presence. Now what?

The roof fell. The Dean informed me I did not have enough credits to graduate with my class. I had to take an extra course and that meant I could not march, in cap and gown, with the rest of the gang from Journalism at the graduation ceremonies.

The disappointment is still vivid. The sense of injustice still rankles. He may have been quite correct in his assessment of my academic record, but why had he not told me before? However, his dictum was final, could not be appealed, and besides there was no time. I was not to graduate with my class.

But I could take a course during the summer session at the university and win my diploma in September. I could select the subject I wished, from a group that I think would now be called the humanities. I chose Modern European History: instructor, Professor J. Salwyn Schapiro. It sounded interesting and would not, I presumed, be a difficult course. History was mostly words and dates and I was a whiz at memorizing dates of battles, lines of succession to the throne, who beat whom and who was the prime minister at the time.

Professor Schapiro was the greatest boon of my student career. He is now a busy, active Professor Emeritus, and may the Lord grant him many more vigorous years!

I knew of the French Revolution, but was not aware of the spreading effect its idea had on the history of other countries. Nor was I aware exactly why General Lafayette had come to the American Colonies to fight in our Revolution. It was a fine gesture on his part, but that it had anything to do with conditions in his own country, or contemporary thought, eluded me. The same went for the American Civil War. I could glibly call off the dates of the big battles and how often the North changed generals, but made no correlation between the industrialization of England and why our domestic tragedy was so pertinent to her national fate. Likewise, the long-lasting effects of Napoleon's bloody and swashbuckling attempts to unite Europe under his own rule meant nothing to me after the Battle of Waterloo. That finished *him* off, and we could go on to a differently-colored part of the map.

In all fairness, perhaps some of my dedicated teachers had tried to present the world as a whole, but if they did I didn't know it. My history instruction had been mostly chronological. In Professor Schapiro's words, "The chronological narrative is confusing in its very simplicity . . . various subjects, although closely related, cannot be clearly understood unless they are disentangled and treated topically." He included social, economic and cultural matters with the military and political. There was a place in his teaching for literary figures. Previously they had been pigeonholed, for me, in literature courses. Now they walked, alive and vibrant, on the stage of "history." How intriguing that socialism (reserved for a minor place in political science) and feminism were factors in determining history!

Such comprehensive history—with due emphasis on concurrent events in different parts of the world, the influence of social thought, as well as wars and dynasties —is standard in college courses today, labeled something like Civilization I and II. But teaching was more compartmentalized in those days.

The course I had started as a martyr's chore soon became an adventure. I knew nothing of the labor movement in the United States; I had never heard of it. That was to come later, in graduate scool, but by then I had the background because I had learned in Professor Schapiro's course of the early stirrings of trade unionism in England and on the Continent, of the horrors of daily life of factory workers in the last century, plus the fact that all this was going on at the same time important things were happening in the United States. Professor Schapiro linked them together in a great chain of world events: the struggle for the unification of Italy and the potato famine in Ireland were no longer isolated wars and catastrophies, but were intimately involved with the history of other parts of the world. This was the revelation.

It was truly a world concept, with national happenings woven like threads into a great multicolored world tapestry.

It would be difficult today for the average thinking person to ignore the immediacy of far-off events to our own personal and national welfare. Americans have consented to be taxed heavily for one of the greatest beneficences ever attempted by man, the rehabilitation of war-stricken countries after World War II. To be sure, opposition exists on the question of foreign aid, and some are irked by the continuing necessity of building up, helping to develop and feeding less fortunate parts of the world. But the commitment is accepted by the majority of Americans. It is only a question of how, and how much, rather than the scrapping of the entire responsibility, that triggers debate in our press and Congress.

But isolation was the pervading philosophy of those days in the 1920's. The rest of the world was not our concern. Even though I regarded myself as being among the enlightened, I had not learned that the cries of a hungry child or the groans of a political prisoner would soon resound, frighteningly near, in our own ears. But I was ready for the lesson that most of us have learned the hard way: Everything reacts on everything else in the world, and it is not instant communication that fuses the woes and wars, politics and philosophies of the world into one vast panorama. It was always so, just that many of us did not know it. Anyway, I didn't know it. Professor Schapiro did.

Art too. Modern art, nonobjective art, with its fragmented presentation of life, became explicable to me even though not always immediately palatable. (Today life itself is fragmented, not only by allegiances and the erosion of many previously taken-for-granted verities, but also by the revelation of scientists that life is broken into many component parts which are all related to the whole, to be sure, but are jagged with jostling and intimidating facts.) I had also learned that literature and art were part of history, that they were molded by current events, and that they in turn helped mold public opinion far outside their particular fields.

Even though not blessed with a keen eye for the graphic arts, I was able to accept the art of the subconscious which showed what the mind's eye perceives, rather than merely being able to accept the standard older forms of exact representation. I can accept modern sculpture, too, even though I still can't quite understand the great, gaping holes in the middle of the figure. All right, this I do know: Life may be discontinuous in parts, and it proceeds in fits and starts, but it does go on in many forms in all parts of the world. I repeat this to myself at such art exhibitions, keeping Professor Schapiro's concomitance firmly in my boggled mind's eye.

Many years later, after that summer school course, I met a Professor Schapiro at the home of the late Professor Theodore Goodman, originator of the famous writing courses at City College which turned out so many of our best contemporary writers. My host told me that Professor Schapiro, a tall, graying, keen-eyed, craggy-featured man, taught history at City College.

"Are you *J. Salwyn* Schapiro?" I queried. He said he was. I informed him that I had studied with him one summer at Columbia University, and. . . . That wasn't possible, he interrupted, as he had always taught at City College and during the summer at the Sorbonne in Paris. I insisted, and he then recollected that yes, he had once given a course in Modern European History at Columbia University summer school. "It was in 1922," I went on, and for further identification I mentioned that there were two marks for the course, one for a final paper and another for regular class work and tests.

"What marks did you get?" he asked.

I replied that I had gotten an A in each. He looked disbelieving, but I was firm. "You must have been a fine student," he concluded.

"I had a very fine professor," I retorted.

✻

ON
REMEMBERING
MONSIEUR DELMAS

Thomas Merton

ON
REMEMBERING
MONSIEUR DELMAS

Thomas Merton

A couple of months ago, in writing an introduction to
the *Letters of Fénelon,* I was reminded of Monsieur
Delmas, because it was from him that I first heard of
Fénelon, a great and sometimes neglected writer of the
French Classical age. Fénelon was himself a teacher—
tutor to the young Duke of Burgundy who, at one
point, looked as if he might inherit the throne of Louis
XIV. If he had done so the history of Europe would
have been very different. It was for this young prince
that Fénelon had written his masterly pedagogical novel
Télémaque. But Fénelon has not always been in favor
with French academic thought; indeed, he even came
under censure at Rome for one of his books. He was a
mystic, and a mystic is necessarily in some respects a
nonconformist, though the gentle and clear intelligence
of Fénelon was not the mind of a rebel.

The reason I bring Fénelon into this is that M. Delmas was an exception: He was a Frenchman who liked

Fénelon. I cannot remember exactly why. Perhaps he just had a temperamental affinity for the great Bishop, though M. Delmas may have been a Calvinist. I do not remember. He was not the kind who would discuss his religion in class.

I suppose I ought to begin at the beginning. This was in 1927, in France. I was twelve and had just entered the Lycée Ingres, at Montauban, which as far as I could see at that time was about equivalent to entering Sing Sing. Although I had been born in France I was not really French, and since I had been out of the country for most of my childhood I had to relearn the language. The French official mind as reflected in a Lycée of the Third Republic was not exactly what I felt to be congenial to my own rather pensive and solitary humors. We led a regimented life, to put it mildly. We were subjected to all kinds of pompous official pronouncements, expected to conform to authoritarian decrees of all sorts, and, apart from that, submerged in an atmosphere of rather humorless austerity against which even the youngest students reacted with profane and (when it was safe) violent tendencies.

The students lived and groaned under a hierarchy of noncelestial beings. At the top of the pyramid was a thin, silent, remote figure: M. le Proviseur. I never really spoke to him until the day I left (in 1928) when I found him to be surprisingly human. After him there was M. le Censeur, whom I don't remember—at least not M. le Censeur of 1927. M. le Censeur of 1928 used to sneak into the dormitory to catch people at their various forms of mischief *in flagrante delicto*. He was a small, narrow-eyed, gendarme type for whom delicts were obviously flaming all the time. Under these two luminaries shone lesser stars upon the groves of academe.

At the bottom of the hierarchy were disciplinary drudges, nicknamed *pions*, who presided over study hall (*permanence*) and took us for walks on Thursdays. These were grim, professionally severe, and probably very frustrated men. They were cordially hated by the students, who insulted them whenever it was feasible but obeyed them with servile or contemptuous fear, depending on the capacity for ruthlessness which each one was able to display. I do not remember these characters with any special pleasure, though I now realize how much they deserved compassion.

The professors seem generally to have been men of a different stamp. They had no contact with the students except in class. They appeared and disappeared. No one knew where they came from or where they went. The only one whose personal life could be discussed in the chilly gravel yards of our penitentiary was the professor of Spanish, who was reputed to be a drunk and who, it was said, sometimes landed in jail. When the students thought this had taken place, they would put an empty violin case on his desk the next time he returned to teach, to see what he would do. The slang for jail, or as we might say, "the tank," was *le violin*. I don't know how he acted when he saw this painful symbol, as I did not take Spanish. I took German, and the red bearded German professor was very popular. He was one of the most friendly men on the faculty, and we knew where he lived because we passed his villa on our walks and saw him high up on the flat roof making meteorological observations, which awakened in our hearts a deep sense of awe.

Most of these professors were all right. They were visibly human. Even the first time you met them, you could see that they were really people and not gendarmes, at least most of them. I cannot remember any that I did not get along with fairly well. They remain in my mind as indistinct and sympathetic shadows, with the exception of the math professor, who taught in a gloomy cavern of a room where no intellectual light of any sort ever glimmered in my mind. He was a spook as well as a bore. Next door was the place where we learned fencing; equally gloomy, if you like, but much more fun.

Mr. Delmas taught French to my class, which was the lowest: *sixième*. This means that we started with the simplest classics—the Fables of La Fontaine, bits of *Télémaque*, I am sure, and the *Characters* of La Bruyers, which I liked. We also had the worst of Racine's plays, which was supposed to be a comedy.

In any case, M. Delmas was a small, decent, unassuming, unobtrusive, smiling type: kind and friendly but definitely discreet. I do not remember him ever getting angry or being impatient. I cannot possibly associate with his person anything like bluster or official bombast, and I think the reason why I liked him was that I fully believed he never said anything he did not mean. This, to my young mind, was rather important. I did not intend then (any more than I have ever intended since) to accept statements that were made as official and as authoritative as possible for the sole reason that the person making them knew on which side his bread was buttered. M. Delmas didn't bring the question of his bread and butter into the scene at all. He dealt with boys as with people, not trying to kid them, as I think American educators are urged to do, that they were *important* people. The French certainly don't encourage children to think that they are able and ready to run the universe as of now. And that was all right with us. But we were glad that M. Delmas at least took us seriously enough at the moments when we had a right to be taken seriously.

One of the things a boy of twelve rightly expects to be understood is that he is no genius, and that the teacher will have to wait a little before getting great results—or any results at all. In other words, the purpose of the student is not merely to provide the teacher with opportunities to be an official success and advance rapidly in his career. The teacher exists for the student, not the other way around.

M. Delmas understood this very well, and he was patient. He was content with even small successes. But he did expect some degree of thought, not just flattery and cajolery. And because he was eminently serious about this, we seriously strove to understand words, sentences and grammatical connections. For a long time I was able to say only what was correct, without being able to explain why. One day, when the theory suddenly dawned on me simply as a different and more technical kind of language (not as a mystery open only to initiates) and when I saw that it was not hard to use this language, M. Delmas was even more pleased than I was. This is an experience I shall not forget, principally because neither of us could lay claim to having accomplished anything special. The light had dawned, and a gift had been given. The professor had simply maintained an atmosphere in which such a gift was possible.

This is the most important thing I can remember about M. Delmas: He helped me to discover that grammar was for men, not men for grammar. Everything else, even if I remembered it, would be little more than accidental. But I think he had the same sort of quality I have always appreciated in all teachers who have really given me something important. (I have written elsewhere about many of these, such as Mark Van Doren and Dan Walsh.) M. Delmas had a certain tact, a humility in the presence of life and of reality. He had discretion. He had taste. He liked what he thought. He did not despise students as such. He took an interest in other human beings. He found human beings more important than regulations, theories, programs, systems and collective prescriptions. Briefly, he was a simple, honest, perhaps fallible human being who did not insist on being taken for anything other than what he was: A man interested in helping young people use the French language with a certain amount of intelligence.

I don't think I ever thanked him, or that he ever expected to be thanked. The next year I went up into *cinquième* and thereafter saw little of M. Delmas, though I remember meeting him once outside the office of the *Censeur* where I was trying to get permission to go downtown to the movies. M. Delmas smiled as though he regarded me as one of his more creditable alumni, now doing well in the academic world of grownup people aged thirteen.

What has happened to him since? Where was he

when the Nazis came to Montauban, where men were hanged in the square in front of the Cathedral, when the bishop protected the resistance fighters? Where was he when the Nazis went away and other dimensions of violence became known? I have no idea. But clearly, M. Delmas (along with Fénelon) has remained, in my mind, a symbol of the best side of France: The tact; the intelligence; the respect for being; the humorous, independent and tolerant view of life; the charity, the culture and the respect for freedom which make up a civilized man.

✳

THE TEACHER
AS EMANCIPATOR

Ann Hatfield

✿✿✿✿✿✿✿✿✿✿✿✿✿✿✿✿✿✿✿✿✿✿✿✿✿✿✿✿✿✿

One of the leading interior designers of the country, chiefly of commercial and public buildings, this contributor is the name partner of Ann Hatfield Associates of New York. When Mount Holyoke made her an honorary Doctor of Fine Arts, it said she had "demonstrated that a creative artist can successfully combine a professional career with the role of wife and mother."

✿✿✿✿✿✿✿✿✿✿✿✿✿✿✿✿✿✿✿✿✿✿✿✿✿✿✿✿✿✿

※

THE TEACHER
AS EMANCIPATOR

Ann Hatfield

The casual and even friendly relationship which my sons enjoy with their instructors is for me incredible. During my high school days and later at Mount Holyoke, teachers were considered to be the enemy, classed roughly with parents and even slightly more suspect. The few people in my group who were reading for honors spent what the rest of us called "social time" with heads of departments, and claimed that these individuals were as funny or as interesting or as queer or perhaps as frightened as we were. We didn't believe this, but occasionally for the sake of our bright friends we did make an effort to treat the monsters as contemporaries.

My particular plight in this regard was especially painful at college because, as president of the class, I was supposed to fraternize cheerfully with those unhappy instructors or professors whom we elected as honorary members. Even now the memory of those fortunately rare occasions makes me cringe.

With this background it astonishes me to realize that I have been married to a very distinguished teacher and bask daily in the warmth of his colleagues' affection, and that I have a particular friend in the teaching profession: Miss Helen Abbott. Forty years after our first meeting, Miss Abbott is still the quintessence of educational excellence.

Why I should think so gives me pause. I feel as though all this should have been resolved years ago in psychoanalysis, but as I remember the hours on the couch, Miss Abbott's name never came up. Let me see if I can now recapture the reasons for her excellence.

In the smug, drab, New England town of Reading, Massachusetts, she shocked parents by taking her English class—there must have been thirty of us, but perhaps not quite all went—thirteen miles away to the theater in Boston at night. The idea that boys and girls might travel to the sinful city together at all, let alone to a play, was pretty daring for the time and place. I know my own parents would never have dreamed of allowing me to join except that they supposed the journey was sponsored by the school.

But this was not the sum of Miss Abbott's uniqueness as a teacher. During school hours she made us read Shakespeare with expression, flailing our arms and actually laughing in class. She took walks with us, explaining in parables that vanity was a fine thing. She permitted us to get the point that it was possible to bathe as often as we liked, add toilet water to our skins, actually enjoy

the company of the opposite sex without feeling like
brazen hussies. She inflated my own sad ego by confusing me with the prettiest girl in class. To my surprise
and delight I became aware of the fact that she really
liked me, and that fact was very important.

The Reading in which I grew up was a small Middlesex town inhabited, so far as I knew, almost entirely by
families whose heads commuted to and from the city on
the old Boston and Maine Railroad. But the families
were as untouched by vast changes then taking place
elsewhere in the country—as I discovered later—as if
they were still living in the nineteenth century. That
their child should dream of anything different was completely unintelligible to them. They were—or seemed
to me—so thoroughly self-satisfied! The houses were so
neat and carefully unostentatious; the village square was
shaded by such fine old elms; the churches were so
numerous and large and well-attended.

Before Miss Abbott, nothing relieved this dismal setting for me. At dancing school, to which all the children
I knew were solemnly herded, I suffered the agonies of
being a shy girl who had the misfortune to be at least a
head taller than any of the boys with whom I danced.
Only unsympathetic stares met my deep but perhaps
frustratedly inarticulate desire to study drawing and
design. In that circle it was quite proper for a young
woman to sketch or dabble in water colors, but surely
she shouldn't think of it as anything more than a pleasant ladylike accomplishment.

And then in my junior year at Reading High School I
sat in Miss Abbott's English class. She was in her middle

thirties then, a product of Reading herself, but I remember thinking she looked foreign somehow. Perhaps it was the light in her bright brown eyes, because really there was nothing very remarkable about her appearance. She had interesting rather than pretty features, an asymmetrical face and brown hair. I do not remember much about her dress except for a string of gold beads; I retain only an impression of a good figure, well-groomed.

I doubt that she meant nearly as much to anyone else in the class as she meant to me. It wasn't only the visits to the theater in Boston and the delightful way she had of making English literature a pleasure that affected me. Miss Abbott thought me too self-effacing and too given to moods of self-hatred, and she tried to help me overcome these deficiencies. The very fact that someone cared enough to try gave a great boost to my morale.

While I don't remember that she was concerned with my yearnings toward a career in the arts, nor that I ever poured them out to her while I was in her classes those last two years in high school, she profoundly influenced my eventual pursuit of such a career. It now seems to me that it was she who laid the groundwork for my fleeing, the minute I graduated from college, from the anathema which was Massachusetts. New York became at once my spiritual home, and for years I never looked backward.

However, Miss Abbott kept cropping up in my life— she had friends in New York. When I had time to lunch with her (45 minutes sometimes), she scolded that my coat was too thin, that I was not getting enough sleep and therefore should not go to the one free art school every night. I said pooh and she went away for three years. The next time we met she was outraged that my husband had not provided me with a fur coat, and insisted on going home with me to see the baby. Five years later, before sailing for Europe, she uncovered in a ten-minute interview all my problems and blamed them briskly on my alma mater.

Long before this, Miss Abbott had ceased to be a teacher and also ceased to be Miss Abbott. Shortly after I left Reading High School, she retired to marry a suitor from Worcester, a widower who had intrigued us for a long time by coming all the way from that distant metropolis to take Miss Abbott out to dinner. So in the intervals between our meetings she was also making a new life—several new lives in fact. She became a house-wife with her own children and stepchildren to care for, but she worked on a newspaper in Worcester as well. Then she had a successful career as a lecturer, and I heard that she had to give it up because the audiences grew too large for the available facilities. She then went on to achieve some reputation as a writer, and today, at 77, she is as alert, as decisive, as illuminating as ever.

Through all the years we have continued to meet in bright little spurts and correspond intermittently, promising each other that some time we would sit down and discuss life at length. Once we almost did. We had made elaborate plans to meet at her house on Cape Cod one winter. My daughter-in-law drove me up, since she lives in Boston, and when we got there Miss Abbott was worried—as indeed we were too—by broadcasts warning of an approaching blizzard which might maroon us there indefinitely. The news cut to two hours what was to have been a weekend, but one of the charms of our relationship is that it really didn't matter. Maybe a weekend would have been too much.

❋

RECALLING DOOB

Tuck Stadler

****

*Maury Tuckerman Stadler is a broad-
caster-writer for WINS, New York's all
news radio station. Before that he covered
many important news and feature stories.
He came to WINS from service as a TV
writer for ABC after eight years of experience as a reporter-newscaster in Oklahoma, the city editorship of* The Independence (*Mo.*) Daily News *and work
on* The Kansas City Star.

****

*

RECALLING
DOOB

Tuck Stadler

It is almost twenty communism-confounding years since we were in Leonard Doob's classes. I phoned three classmates to ask what they recalled of him. My accountant friend remembered:

"I got from him the habit of listening first and not taking notes until later. You had to stay on your toes, and finally the structure of what he was saying would come through, like a sort of hero of that day's lecture-story. He made statistics livable for me, for the first time."

A writer, who'd grown up in the Yale community, remembered an incident:

"He had small children at the time and he worked at home so hard on his lectures and books. To override the kids' screams and squeals, he'd set up a noisemaker in his home. I think it was watchman's rattles, attached to an electric fan, to clatter above the kids' sounds. But in his lectures, his theory of values came through to me. I saw for the first time that societies changed and you couldn't predict what values would change or survive. It was quite a change from hard and fast notions I got at Groton."

An editor recalled:

"Most of my Yale teachers in the social sciences in those days bored me, but Doob was unjargonized—he didn't use ludicrous jargon for the obvious. He was like an essayist or journalist and always made his lectures lively and imaginative."

Did a Merriwell-era idealism or naïveté still exist in Yale College from 1946 to 1948, my two years there? I nearly laugh to recall going to the Shubert Theater one night to watch an unknown actor, Marlon Brando, play in unknown writer Tennessee Williams' *A Streetcar Named Desire*. The crude Stan who he played angered me with his immorality in seducing his sister-in-law (wasn't it?) while his wife gave birth to their child! In those days, we would argue for our beliefs: Price control, aid to Greece and Turkey, Taft conservatism and Wallace progressivism *mattered!* We got angry or enthusiastic over them. I declined Yale President Charles Seymour's invitation to give to the Community Chest until he assured me, which he did in a short note, that Jews weren't admitted to the University by quota. Arguing in the Saybrook dining hall about Negroes one day, we got so excited that a future banker with whom I disagreed suggested we discontinue the subject "in a public place."

Today's student, according to my impression, isn't less idealistic but is more realistic, and if you wonder out loud if Maury Wills is a Negro, he looks askance at you for your irrelevance.

Some of us sought heroes, and Yale undergraduates thronged to the classrooms of a sociologist named Kennedy who daily damned the University's quaint customs. They also crowded the lectures of an English historian named Driver. I knew neither of these teachers. My deity was Doob, the little associate professor of social psychology who had been one of the founders in the 1930's of *Propaganda Analysis*, a journal that my pacifist mother and I hoped would lead the nation, maybe the world, away from wars. I could hardly wait for my first class with him in my junior year of 1946–1947.

When he came into the classroom in a brown tweed suit, his arms loaded with books, we saw a sort of pointed chin and nose and sharp dark eyes. He'd begin putting mysterious words or diagrams on the blackboard. He'd chat, smilingly, with a student or two until time to begin lecturing. He looked like a mechanism designed to flash out and nail down knowledge.

Unlike Yale's other psychology department luminaries, such as John Dollard with his plodding Midwestern delivery or the grandfatherly, reputation-enshrouded Arnold Gesell, Doob was all action and activity. His one-syllable name was appropriately brisk, but its connotation could have been made more spry: "Zoop" or "Boom" or "Zoom" might have been closer. But he was "Doob" and he was great.

As he began to speak, in a precise, clear manner, it seemed to me I heard the faintest residue of another language's influence, as if he'd grown up in a home where two languages were spoken. I learned this might have been from his having studied at Frankfurt am Main after being graduated with honors from Dartmouth, though Doob looked unlike my big, blond, skiing concept of a Dartmouth man. A classmate told me Doob had a Czech-American heritage. Fairly fresh from having fought Nazis, I thought of Doob's having studied propaganda under the same professors as Joseph Paul Goebbels, who was evidently bright, too, in his fearsome way and had rather thin features, quite like Doob's own. It never occurred to me that Doob might be one of the Jewish good guys, which I was later told he was. He seemed sort of raceless, unattached ethnically and coolly scientific.

Doob expected his students to be alert and attentive and brighter than people I was used to dealing with. I found myself, in our occasional bits of conversation, trying to seem more intelligent than I believed myself to be. My laboratory partner and I were to consult him in his office in the Institute of Human Relations to outline our term project. My classmate conceived it as a study of anti-Semitism among undergraduates, which we suspected was fairly rampant among the socialite students. But Doob wouldn't accept this, or any hunches ahead of evidence. We had to stretch our interviewing plans to prove that we'd be getting reliable results that would actually add something to the literature of our field. How it thrilled us a year or so later to learn that some of our findings were quoted in class in an offhand manner by another teacher, in the tone of, "Allport's findings at Harvard and Brunswik-Franke's at California were partly confirmed by the study of Edens and Stadler at Yale, in finding . . ."!

But his standards were stiff in the random picking of students we'd interview and how to get their honest feelings. He suggesed some control techniques to guard against invalid results. Both in the classroom and in these counseling or tutorial sessions, it seemed to me that Doob was always one step ahead of the student. He knew what you were thinking and you couldn't dazzle him. He once spoke of an experience that apparently recurred in his association with students: An under-graduate would ask him, ostensibly in behalf of a room-mate or friend, how a student could get a bit of psycho-therapy, Doob commenting that it was obvious the young man was covertly trying to arrange for such treatment or guidance for himself. What brave Yaley would let it be known that *he* needed analysis!

In those postwar years, the *Yale Daily News* began putting out critiques on the faculty, a practice later widely copied on American campuses. Doob got high ratings.

My three roommates were chic, conservative chaps from Eastern prep schools or suburbs. I was a coarse, liberal Midwesterner. I defended Truman, they Robert Taft (Yale 1915). I attacked *Herald Tribune* editorials, with which they usually agreed. They chided me for devotion to *PM* and the *St. Louis Post-Dispatch*. I let my sour grapes show and ridiculed Yale societies and architecture. For a few months, I cheered for opposing teams at athletic contests. My roommates wore white shoes and belonged to Mory's. I accused Yale of phony snobbism and prejudice. Doob's standards were a challenge to prove this. Sure enough, our study showed prejudice much lower than my friend and I had expected. I think Doob gave us a B-plus or A-minus on it.

The next year Doob was giving his propaganda course. I didn't always understand his lectures when he got into the complications of linguistics, but they usually began to make sense after a bright classmate, like Arthur Hadley, a former Yale president's grandson, engaged him in a sort of argument. I was anxious to shine on my term paper because my examination grades always hovered in the middle of the class marks. My thesis was to be a measurement of the impartiality of various newspapers.

Life wasn't so computerized then, and to do the study without the personal prejudices of the tester showing through was going to be a tough assignment. Doob's brow furrowed in skepticism, but he let me go ahead. I began measuring the amount of space given to the two sides of controversial issues in five papers, *The New York Times, Chicago Tribune, St. Louis Post-Dispatch* (which I somehow knew would come out most honest and honorable), *The Christian Science Monitor* and, on Doob's suggestion, the *Daily Worker*. It was to be limited to their front pages and to continue for a month. I think the issues included the Truman Doctrine, Henry Wallace, the Chinese Revolution perhaps, and a couple of others, rather clearly dividable into a liberal and a conservative advocacy.

Doob suggested two approaches, one to keep the other from getting out of hand, and off I went to Sterling Library for a month of line-counting and, yes, some interpreting. The results surprised me. The *Times* came out well, but the *Monitor* came out as only *fairly* well balanced. The *Worker* did badly, of course, and the *Post-Dispatch* came out disappointingly, about tied with the detested, conservative *Chicago Tribune!*

When I got my paper back from Doob, he'd written a little note on it, saying, "I didn't think you could pull this off, but it isn't bad." He rated it about B-minus.

In my final term of senior year, I took Doob's Social Psychology and worked hard for occasional A's on exams, but often got only B's or C's and ended with a B. After learning that I was barely in the upper half of his class of two hundred or so students, and concluding that it could not now seem that I was trying to kowtow to a prof to improve my grade, I summoned my self-confidence and invited Doob to lunch in Saybrook College, my residential hall. It was about my last day at Yale; most other students had gone home, and I was waiting for a boat to Europe. Over our metal trays, an unYaley barbarism still hanging over from the War, we talked of his days in Frankfurt and Hanover (N.H.) and New Haven and I kept trying to think of some way to impress him, some more profound observation than he believed me capable of thinking. Finally he stuck out his hand for farewell and said: "If I can ever do anything for you, write a letter of recommendation or anything, be sure and let me know."

That somehow hurt. It made me feel Doob had thought I was trying to forward myself in the world, with his help. It was actually only his own approval that I greatly wanted.

＊

A TEACHER'S
IMMORTALITY

DeWitt Stetten, Jr.

※※※※※※※※※※※※※※※※※※※※※※※

Dean of the new Medical School at Rutgers University, DeWitt Stetten, Jr. is a biochemist who headed the research into arthritis and metabolic diseases for the National Institutes of Health. Before that he had done distinguished work at the Public Health Research Institute in New York and Peter Bent Brigham Hospital in Boston. Born in New York, he was educated at Harvard and Columbia University's College of Physicians and Surgeons and has served on the faculties of both institutions. He has been the recipient of many of the most highly prized awards in his field, including the Banting Medal of the American Diabetes Association.

※※※※※※※※※※※※※※※※※※※※※※※

*

A TEACHER'S
IMMORTALITY

DeWitt Stetten, Jr.

I first met Rudolph Schoenheimer in the winter of
1931. I was entering my second year at Columbia Medical School; he was returning to Germany after a few
months' stay as visiting lecturer in Chicago. A mutual
friend, Erwin Brand of Columbia University, brought
him to supper at my home because Rudi urgently
needed some solid German diet and we chanced to have
a competent German cook.

During and after the *Sauerbraten mit Kartoffelpuffer*,
I had my first exposure to Rudi's unquestioned bril-
liance and his equally clear hypomania. We conspired at
that time that I should spend the following summer in
Freiburg in Breisgau where Rudi, as biochemist to the
Pathologisches Institut of Geheimrat Ludwig Aschoff,
occupied the top floor of that historic laboratory.

The two months which I spent in Freiburg in the
summer of 1932 convinced me that the life in the laboratory was for me. Rudi at that time was single, very

sensitive to the coming political storm and then, as always, anxious to discuss his anxieties. Since in those days of the rise of Hitler it was unsafe to discuss such problems with German colleagues, I became his chief audience. Then, with the elections of August 1932 coming up, Rudi insisted that I get close to the frontier, on the Lake of Constance. He did agree, however, that upon the completion of my medical studies I should return to Freiburg for graduate work in biochemistry.

But it did not work out that way. By December 1932 Rudi was in New York where he found opportunities to work at Columbia University, and within a few months he had settled in the United States. In the years that followed I saw much of the Schoenheimers (Rudi meanwhile had married) while I got my M.D. degree and interned for two and a half years at Bellevue Hospital. I then entered the graduate school of Columbia University and earned my Ph.D. under Rudi's preceptorship.

To an unusual degree Rudi was an intuitive scientist. His students were continuously impressed by his apparent foreknowledge of experimental results. His selection of experiments was remarkably assured, and he made few blunders. He was the first biochemist to realize the full potential of the isotope techniques which he did so much to develop.

The importance of this achievement can be expressed only in a slightly technical explanation. Isotopes are variations of the abundant elementary forms which differ from the more frequent variants in mass and which are frequently radioactive. Their use was introduced by Dr. Schoenheimer into study of biochemical problems. It was found possible to label molecules of interest to the biochemist by replacing the normal abundant atom of one or another element by its isotopic variant and then following the course of that isotope through its metabolic alteration. This method has today become one of the keystone methods of biochemical research and had its origins in Rudi's laboratory.

It was one of his great strengths in research that he had no difficulty in shedding preconceptions due to the work or ideas of others, and replacing these with bold hypotheses of his own design. A man of great intellectual energy and enthusiasm, he transferred these attributes to his close associates in the laboratory.

After work was done he could on occasion relax, but even under these circumstances he was always at the focus of attention, as when he would conduct us through the numerous verses of the song:

> *Die bunte Kuh*
> *Macht manchmal "Muh"*

This is typical of the interminable nonsense jingles which were developed for the merriment of the beer halls and student assemblages of pre-Hitler Germany. It might be translated roughly as:

> *Cows of any hue*
> *Sometimes go "Moo"*

Rudi took his work in science very seriously. Each paper to be prepared for publication was an ordeal for him and for his coauthors. Endless arguments directed toward the choice of the most precise word or the elimination of possible ambiguity often frayed the nerves of collaborators, but Rudi's exuberant goodwill would usually smooth ruffled feathers.

Important as were his papers, his graduate students were even more so. These he alluded to as his "immortality," and to this childless man these were his children. He worried over their personal as well as their educational problems. The ties were very close.

The graduate students who became symbols of Rudi's immortality are now scattered widely throughout the country. For example, Dr. Norman Weissman is at the Utah College of Medicine's Department of Pathology where, among other things, he carries on research in the metabolism of isotopic amino acids. Marjorie Anchel of the New York Botanical Gardens has done notable work in the chemistry and biogenesis of fungal products. Frederick Barnes at Brown University is known for such studies as those in protein regeneration and reaction after harmful stimuli. Marjorie Roloff, who later became my wife, is still another symbol of Rudi's immortality. All of these scientists have continued in their careers the study of intermediary metabolism, and all of them have been enormously influenced by what they learned and did while working with Dr. Schoenheimer.

✻

FOUR
TEACHERS

Conrad Aiken

A product of the South (Savannah) and of Harvard, Conrad Aiken became one of America's most distinguished poets and critics, but is also well known for his short stories and novels. He has received a great many of the literary world's most sought after awards and honors, including the Pulitzer Prize for Poetry in 1929.

✳

FOUR
TEACHERS

Conrad Aiken

The first of my teachers I'd like to tell about must of course be the first teacher I ever had: She was Mrs. Anne Waring, who taught me history and English at Morton's School for Boys in Savannah, Georgia, a private school, not very large, and never famous for its scholarship. Morton himself, the engaging and mustachioed proprietor, made himself memorable by mounting the platform for our opening Latin class, pointing a finger at a lump in his cheek, and asking *"Quid est hoc?"* He then answered the question by rolling the lump into the other cheek and saying *"Hoc est quid."*

Unforgettable, certainly.

But Anne Waring was unforgettable in quite another way, for she was, in the eyes of a boy of eleven, not only exquisitely beautiful—a fact to which photographs which I acquired many years later still testify—but also gentle, perceptive and, when occasion demanded (as for example when we tethered June bugs to our desks with a thread), firm.

I worshiped her but without knowing it. She had sons who were older than I, and obviously she knew exactly what to do with an inordinately shy boy who was, in a "social" sense, still curiously unadapted and incompetent. (I might add that much later in my life I came to know the whole family and to learn that she was regarded by all of Savannah as a heroic figure.) Anyway, she knew better than to disparage the bad drawing I made from a picture of Julius Caesar in the history book, and which I ventured to take up to her desk.

And what I have always thought was the real turning point of my life came one day when, in the small classroom, after an expression of aggrieved disappointment in our work, she turned, looked at me and said, "I think *Conrad* will someday amount to something."

This accolade changed my life in an instant. It gave me the self-belief and courage which I hadn't hitherto had, and a purpose and center, too. Who can possibly weigh the consequences of such an action? Incalculable, at any rate, they were for me, and it grieves me that I was never able to tell her so. It was more than thirty years before I was to return to Savannah, and by then she was many years dead. But I could and did tell her children and grandchildren, I am happy to say.

A great teacher? Certainly not in the accepted sense of the word. But if we remember the Latin derivation of the word *education*—a drawing forth, an evocation— she was indeed a great teacher for me.

Others, later, were to become heroes in other ways: Archibald Victor Galbraith, at Middlesex School, who taught me so much more than mathematics and Kipling and soccer. He had the wisdom and kindness to know how to save a boy's broken pride after a public humiliation—the pride of a boy who, without warning, at a hastily summoned board meeting, was demoted from the editorship of the school paper—and for this I can say that I *have* had the opportunity to thank him, and to add that he had been my hero all my life, my image of what a man should be.

And finally, those two wonderful geniuses at Harvard, the saint and the satyr: Dean LeBaron Russell Briggs, the angel of a composition course, English 5, which I was allowed to take twice, such a miracle of revelation it was, and such a miracle he; and last of all George Santayana, "Santy," whose course on Three Philosophical Poets, and tea-time seminar on Shelley, helped me to set *my* course, and to civilize it, if I may put it so.

These are the people to whom I owe most; a debt that can never be repaid.

✳

A
REMEMBERED
GLOW

Caroline K. Simon

Lawyer, publicist, expert on crime prevention and the work of women's and children's courts, Caroline K. Simon served with distinction as member of or legal counsel to many important boards and commissions, and as Secretary of State of New York. She is now a Judge of the State's Court of Claims and Chairman of the National Council on Crime and Delinquency.

A
REMEMBERED
GLOW

Caroline K. Simon

There is so much that is exciting about learning that when Morris Ernst asked me who had influenced me most among the teachers I immediately responded it was my parents. Through them I had learned to have eyes open and seeing, and mind alert to the wonders of the world. But Morris told me that parents and spiritual leaders were not going to be permitted as "favorite teacher" of any of his contributors, and he asked me about those I had encountered at some level of formal education.

I then told him, as I am happy now to write, about the teacher of English I had at Columbia University. I hope that the teacher will learn here from one of his students how much he meant and for how long a time he has been admired and remembered. He was Mr. Foley to his class, and I have no recollection of his first name, if indeed I ever knew it.

At the time I was living at 353 Garden Avenue,

Mount Vernon (then largely a residential suburb of New York City with even more tree-shaded streets than it has now, but with only a small fraction of its present population). I had just graduated from Mount Vernon High School, and I was fifteen years old.

I had won a Regents scholarship, for which one didn't then compete except by taking the Regents examination, and had expected to go away to college. But during the preceding year my parents decided that I could not carry out this plan. The daughter of a friend of theirs had died in her freshman year at college in another city, and they felt that any program of mine for pursuing studies far from home would have to be changed. That decision brought me to Columbia University and what was then known as the Department of Extension Teaching, now called the School of General Studies.

There I enrolled for a course in freshman English, and no question of my youth was raised. The students in that Department were, as those in its successor School are now, a broad cross section of the intellectually curious people of New York City and adjoining counties. They were of all ages, from very young pre-freshmen like myself to grandparents and even great-grandparents. The ordinary academic requirements demanded of regularly matriculated students were waived because the aim of the Department was to offer opportunity for college-level study, although without college credit, to men and women who had a genuine desire to learn.

The class I attended as a day student was listed as freshman English. It could have been called Logic, or

Thinking or any one of a number of titles because what it really taught was evaluation, analyzation and consideration. No course could be more helpful to a lawyer and a judge. However, in a free society everyone needs to have such training so that he will not just read and accept, but read and think: Is this all there is to know on this subject? Is there some other aspect? Is the development from the principles to the concepts sound?

I was fifteen and my teacher may have been in his early twenties, a poet who gave us the beauty of listening to and reading poetry that throbbed and sang. There was such test of meaning that it was a living experience which would continue to give its glow and its beauty to the whole of our lives.

Did I ever say "thank you" to him, you ask? Not really, unless this can be considered a "thank you" long, long after the happening. But that class came eager to its room, was attentive and participating, a most responsive group, and all this must have given him a sense that he was reaching the people he was teaching. That in itself must have been his reward.

Though his class did not make me choose the law as a career, there being other factors that impelled my choice, his teaching did help me analyze statements, weigh them and make my own judgments.

Perhaps because my own mother was a teacher, I came early to have a respect for teachers. I know that there is no profession more essential in democracy, so I have many times tried to say my thanks to Mr. Foley and my parents by accepting invitations from teachers' groups to speak. The stimulus of Mr. Foley's teaching has remained vibrant to this day. Because of my respect for teachers, I am very glad that I am, at least, an honorary member of a teaching sorority, Delta Kappa Gamma, and have been nominated as an international honorary member.

Probably no real teacher gets to hear verbal thanks from his students. But he knows when there is someone to whom he is communicating his own excitement about learning. He knows it from the interested faces. He knows it from the quiet of the classroom. He knows it from the preparation given to assignments. He knows it from the questions asked of him. And he knows it in many other more subtle ways.

To such a teacher advancement sometimes means only removal to an administrative post where the whole glow of his skill is deadened. If we could have each real teacher know that his worth in our society is recognized, perhaps more of them would keep at their tasks to the everlasting benefit of us all.

✳

A
CAREER
IS BORN

Reginald Heber Smith

❊❊❊❊❊❊❊❊❊❊❊❊❊❊❊❊❊❊❊❊❊❊❊❊❊❊❊

Reginald Heber Smith held the post into which the teacher of whom he writes here thrust him for only four years, but he remained a pillar of legal aid work for half a century before his death in 1966. His book, Justice and the Poor, *to which he refers, has been a classic in its field since 1919, and in 1959 the National Legal Aid Association established the Reginald Heber Smith medal in his honor.*

❊❊❊❊❊❊❊❊❊❊❊❊❊❊❊❊❊❊❊❊❊❊❊❊❊❊❊

A
CAREER
IS BORN

Reginald Heber Smith

Teachers have played a great part in my life. I owe
them so much that I have tried to repay a part of my
indebtedness by doing, I believe and hope, what would
please them most—by being a teacher myself. When
trying to teach, I always had them in mind.

At Harvard College I was an instructor in Public
Speaking 3; I had a class in English at the Prospect
Union (in Central Square, Cambridge) and, at the
school in Roxbury conducted by the Boston Central
Labor Union, a course on law.

As for my own teachers, in the Fall River (Mass.)
Public High School, when I was sixteen, Miss Winward
not only taught me the French language but also how to
pronounce it. This was sufficiently unusual to be
marked down in a book of gratitude.

And then there was also the extraordinary Miss Julia
Amanda Reed. She always dressed demurely in black.
That included a black shirtwaist with a black collar and

black tie. As she taught us Latin declensions and the pronunciation of *veni, vidi, vici,* she used the blackboard. By the time the session was over, her necktie was twisted around in the back; white chalk marks were all over her clothes; and a light was in her eyes as it is in the eyes of all those who devote their lives to what Bliss Perry called "the happy profession." As a student of Latin I was definitely on the dumb side, but when I was married I sent her an invitation and she responded with the gift of a fine book.

And now I come to the extraordinary and tragic Ezra Ripley Thayer. He was Dean of the Harvard Law School from 1910 to 1915, a position to which he had just been appointed at the age of 44, when I entered the institution.

The heart of the Harvard Law School is Langdell Hall. On its pediment are engraved in stone the names of some of its great teachers—Story, Langdell, Williston, Beale, Thayer. But that last is not Ezra; it is his father, James Bradley Thayer, whose fame is perpetuated by his extraordinary treatise, *The Rule Against Perpetuities.* In his introduction he wrote (in substance) that there was something so devilish about the rule—in which America rejected the idea that a man could be permitted to tie up his estate forever so far as his descendants were concerned—that it could always trip up every lawyer including himself. James Bradley Thayer had served under both Dean Langdell, who revolutionized legal education by introducing the case method of study, and Dean Ames, who carried that revolution forward. The son, Ezra Ripley Thayer, certainly showed every evidence of having absorbed the best of the pedagogical traditions from this background.

However, in his early professional life he had had no interest in teaching, and in fact resisted it for many years, refusing several invitations to join the faculty. The first of these offers was no doubt made to him as his father's son, but soon they were extended to him in his own right as a man who had reached a position of leadership at the Boston bar. So when he did accept, he came to the Law School at the top, as its Dean after the death of Ames, and at the same time as a professor of evidence and torts. It was said that he assumed this dual role with some hesitation, but certainly so far as we students ever could see there was nothing in the least hesitant about the way he flung himself into the work.

He had a record of great distinction. After his graduation from the Law School he speedily established a highly successful practice in Boston. For a few years in the late 1890's he had been one of the junior partners of the future Supreme Court Justice Louis D. Brandeis, who had studied under his father. Their association remained close and friendly enough that when a storm of protest was raised against President Woodrow Wilson's nomination of Brandeis to the Supreme Court in 1913, Dean Thayer was one of the few among the "Brahmins" who came to his defense. His letter to the President's adviser was in the sharp, dictatorial manner he used when giving directions to a favorite student: "Lots of the talk which is going about concerning him is rubbish or worse."

In his office he had been altogether devoted to his

work, as he later became in the classroom. He was especially esteemed among idealistic students for the leading part he took in drafting the national code of legal ethics as a member of the American Bar Association's committee appointed for that purpose.

So great was his sense of duty that when he succeeded Ames in 1910 he gave up the practice of law entirely. In 1913 he even refused appointment to a seat on the supreme judicial court of Massachusetts because he felt that his life and energies were committed to his faculty and his students.

Thayer was an exceptionally handsome man and had a reputation in the Boston and Cambridge drawing rooms of his day as a fascinating conversationalist. It was said that his charming talk was the fruit of his lifelong love of the Greek and English classics, which he read and reread with avidity. A few of his students were additionally impressed because his mother had been Ralph Waldo Emerson's cousin. Emerson used to give readings in the Thayer home in Ezra's youth, for that home was then one of the haunts of Boston culture.

I myself took only one course from him, his famous one on evidence and torts. It was a large class, as all were in that day, with perhaps 200 students enrolled. He was fully as fascinating a lecturer as his reputation for social conversation would lead one to expect, but for students he was a bit awesome, not to say frightening, as well.

Here is a little story about him as a teacher. In my law school class of 1914, one of my best friends was Louis Seelbach, and a splendid man he was. (He had played on the football team at Center College, Kentucky, and told us how great it was. We assumed he was bragging.

A few years later Center College came to Cambridge, played against Harvard in the Stadium and won handily —probably the most famous upset of a big "football power" by a little unknown in the history of the sport.)

This day in the classroom, Professor Thayer called on Louis to report on the case involving Lord Leonard's will. The evidence of the barrister's clerk was involved. When Louis responded and said *clerk* in our American pronunciation, Thayer told him rather sharply:

"Don't you know that any English barrister would say 'clark'!"

The reproof would hardly be worth the telling, nor the remembering, except for the sequel which was typical of Thayer's meticulous fairness and explains the respect in which his students held him for all his crustiness. The next morning Louis received a letter from Thayer which he showed me. It said:

"Yesterday in class I was oversharp with you. Please accept my apology."

I knew him as Dean better than as teacher, but it was the combination of both that makes him live so vividly in memory after more than half a century. At the end of my second year he sent for me and said:

"Smith, I know that you work each summer in the office of the Boston Legal Aid Society. Also I know that on graduation you will be asked to become General Counsel of the Boston Legal Aid Society. I want you to take that job. Legal Aid is not understood. I know your background and your inheritance. In your third year, cut Constitutional Law. You can read up on that. Take Roscoe Pound's course on Sociological Jurisprudence."

I obeyed to the letter every word of Dean Thayer's

advice. I never saw him after my graduation and so could not thank him in person, but if you believe in immortality as I do, then Ezra Thayer knows about my contribution to this book and knows it is an expression of my gratitude.

It is impossible, of course, to estimate how many others he influenced as he did me. Often men are not aware of such influences until later in life, and even then do not talk about them. But I am convinced that many were directed into paths which they might not have found without him.

His effect upon us was perhaps inevitable given his conception of his duty as head of the Law School. He believed he must know every student so well that he could intelligently help and guide that man in deciding what to do after graduation. With more than a thousand students that task was impossible, but he tried and I believe that he gave his life for it.

He was a virile man and despised weakness in anyone, so that perhaps he was more severe upon himself and inclined to see weakness where there was really only weariness. But even so, what follows is inexplicable.

He had a house in Cambridge and a summer place in Duxbury. He was going to Duxbury one day in September 1915, but he was a minute or two late at the Back Bay Station and missed his train. Something snapped in his brain. Deliberately he walked the four blocks which brought him to the Charles River. He resolutely continued that walk until the water was over his head and he was drowned.

Let all of us bow our heads for a moment. The human brain may be God's greatest creation thus far, but it is always in a delicate and precarious balance. We cannot know what the morrow will bring; all we can do is pray that sanity may not depart from us. The tragic death of Ezra Thayer often haunts me in moments which all of us sometimes experience, and I think of the old truism, "There but for the grace of God go I."

I have perhaps left the impression that this tribute to Ezra Thayer is the only means I have taken to show my appreciation of the role that this truly great man played in my life. But there are two rather more tangible expressions of my gratitude. One is my book, *Justice and the Poor*, which grew out of the specialized career upon which he launched me. The other, which means even more to me, is a beautiful bronze plaque of Dean Thayer which I was instrumental in having placed in the office of the Boston Legal Aid Society and which is an engraving of his face with its splendid features. Underneath is the simple inscription, "A Minute of Justice."

He left me years ago, but his influence will abide with me always.

※

A
TEACHING
TRINITY

E. B. White

✸✸✸✸✸✸✸✸✸✸✸✸✸✸✸✸✸✸✸✸✸✸✸✸✸✸✸✸✸✸

This contribution is appropriately brief; it was written by E. B. White, who perfected those short "Talk of the Town" comments in The New Yorker, *of which he has been a contributing editor since its inception. He is also the author of a dozen volumes notable for the quality of the writing and the urbanity of his style.*

✸✸✸✸✸✸✸✸✸✸✸✸✸✸✸✸✸✸✸✸✸✸✸✸✸✸✸✸✸✸

A
TEACHING
TRINITY

E. B. White

There was one in grammar school, there was one in high school, and there was one in college. All three, I now perceive, were possessed of spirit, and it was the spirit, not the mind, that distinguished them from other teachers. I feel in their debt. School is not an easy time for most scholars who, like mariners, are always on the lookout for some aid to navigation.

All of the teachers in my grammar school were females, and all but one were spinsters. It was the married teacher, Mrs. Schuyler, who lit the fuse for me. She played piano for assembly. She was rather pretty. And when she taught something, or did something, she threw herself into it, carrying me (and I think others) along with her. She must have enjoyed the gift of life, and when, at Thanksgiving time, she played "The breaking waves dashed high," the waves broke, the woods against a stormy sky their giant branches tossed. I was in love with Mrs. Schuyler. I was delighted when she entered a room, felt let down when she left. I remember little else about her. But I still hear the waves break on the stern and rockbound coast of those difficult years.

In high school, where I arrived every morning on my bicycle, there was Miss Bertha Brown. She taught English, and I think I did not encounter her until my junior or senior year. I was, by that time, a professional writer, with both the silver badge and the gold badge of the St. Nicholas League to prove it. I had little interest in literature but was working away at expressing my own thoughts on paper, which I considered adequate for any occasion. Miss Brown, it turned out, liked to read English ballads to the class, and she did so with spirit. She may have fancied herself as a performer (there is something of the exhibitionist in most teachers), but at any rate, when she started to read, the poem took off, and I took off with it. I was amazed at this turn of events and was surprised that a teacher could do this with English verse. I gained a new feeling about letters, a new excitement about the language—its vitality, its variety, and its power. Miss Brown did not educate me in literature or in English, but she made me want to continue my experiments.

At Cornell I met Bristow Adams, who was also a person of spirit. I was lonely and homesick as a freshman, and my own spirit flagged. Professor Adams and his wife, I discovered, received a few students into their house every Monday evening, to sit around and talk. I joined the group and was restored to health. The professor was a man of many talents, and the talent for friendship was among them. I learned, after a bit, that he was under fire: some members of the faculty felt that

he was going too far in cultivating the society of undergraduates, that a certain aloofness is indispensable. Be
that as it may, in his home I felt a confirmation of my
aspirations, a sympathy for my prejudices. I felt encouraged. And I still feel grateful.

*

EXTRACURRICULAR

Henry Dreyfuss

An industrial designer of international prominence, Henry Dreyfuss has won a great many awards and honors including the Architectural League's Gold Medal and election as Benjamin Franklin Fellow of the Royal Society of Arts. Chairman of the Industrial Designers Society of America, he is Professor in Residence at the University of California in Los Angeles and is both teacher and trustee at the California Institute of Technology. But he has also been one of the leading designers of the American theater, and this reminiscence tells how that phase of his career all began.

EXTRACURRICULAR

Henry Dreyfuss

No one who attended the Ethical Culture Schools at any time during the first thirty-odd years of the century could help but be influenced by Emma Mueden.

Officially, Emma Mueden had some classes in literature, but most of her time was well spent preparing those wonderful festivals for which the school was justly famous. A single production might have several hundred children in its cast—the script, the music, the chorus, the direction and, *very* important, the making of all those costumes were Emma Mueden's responsibility and joy. Whenever I think of Emma Mueden she is up to her elbows in green dye—turning long winter underwear into tights for elves.

I never had a class with Emma Mueden, but when I was 15 or 16 and had just enrolled in the Ethical Culture Schools, I was allowed to design scenery for her: everything from *Prometheus Bound* to a pageant for *Cinderella.* The Meeting House where these festivals were held was enormous and no member of the cast ever measured more than four feet two—so the background had to fill the hall and yet be in scale to our fledgling actors. With a magical quality, Emma Mueden made the effort of these spectacles a joy.

Later when I was swept into the turmoil of doing settings for Broadway productions, I looked back to marvel at the serenity of those rehearsals at Ethical. Actually there was very little difference in a dress rehearsal where Emma Mueden presided and a similar time of turmoil before the opening of a play on Broadway. The rehearsal for *Cinderella* or *Prometheus* in the Ethical Culture School auditorium on West 64th Street held all the blood, sweat and tears of the Broadway production of *The Last Mile* or *The Cat and the Fiddle*, and of all the many shows that I eventually worked on in the professional theater. But when Emma Mueden took charge there was never a raised voice; always patience and understanding. The play and production never suffered from this forbearance either.

(The Ethical Culture Schools remain today in the same location in New York, just west of Central Park. The neighborhood has witnessed several metamorphoses, ending up with the construction of Lincoln Center nearby. But Ethical Culture Schools always drew students from every part of the city, and it was here that the educational pioneering associated with the name of the Ethical Culture Movement originated. One of the pioneering ventures was the sort of self-expression for small children exemplified in the stage productions here described.)

Emma Mueden never looked like a schoolmarm of tradition. She dressed in the height of fashion—perhaps purchasing her wardrobe abroad each summer when she took a group of young ladies on "the grand tour."

When I was 17 Emma Mueden somehow learned that I had never attended a concert in Carnegie Hall, and as a surprise for me she procured two tickets up near the roof. None of my subsequent visits to that temple of music has ever produced the thrill of that great moment provided by a great lady. And she was my "date" for the occasion, too.

With careful saving, I had arranged a trip to Europe the year I finished school. Aboard ship I found a letter from Emma Mueden which I shall always treasure, and a five pound note was enclosed—a deprivation for her, I am sure. It was for some "extra" for me on my first trip abroad.

Today when one meets "old grads" of Ethical Culture Schools, Emma Mueden's name always creeps into the conversation, for she inspired and influenced everyone who crossed the threshold of the school. And she always did this with a quiet insistence that the best of ambitions was none too good. She made one shoot for the moon when that was a figurative, not a literal, phrase.

We never lost trace of one another; she knew our children well and they adored her. One Sunday in New York one of my young daughters and I telephoned Emma and asked her to lunch. We called for her in a horse-drawn Victoria and drove down Park Avenue. It was a fine day, and Emma Mueden was kept busy acknowledging the surprised waves of the astounded promenaders, many of whom she knew. What a time she had!

Europe was her favorite stamping ground, and she managed to visit it one way or another every single summer holiday. During the years while she was teaching, she shepherded girl students around the Continent —and what an enriching experience for them! She knew the most obscure things about the most obscure places; old gray walls were made to breathe their romance once again.

In later years, after her retirement, Europe still beckoned—occasionally we would meet there and have a day together. There was an unforgettable drive in Chartres with Emma Mueden, and she shared her knowledge of the history of the town and its great cathedral. My eyes could appreciate the glories of the stone and glass, but she gave that great building a heart and warmth.

These are my own still-cherished "private classes" with Emma Mueden. But students in her formal classes were influenced to an even greater degree, for she bred in them a love of literature, learning and all of the beautiful things available for those who reach a bit further than the rest.

Well, here is one student who will be everlastingly grateful for her interest and friendship—and particularly for one additional reason. Emma Mueden introduced me to my wife.

✳

A
TEACHER
OUT-OF-DOORS

Kay Halle

A
TEACHER
OUT-OF-DOORS

Kay Halle

More than any of my teachers, Maude Alice Doolittle, who taught first grade in a Brookline, Massachusetts public school, made a lasting imprint on my life. She spent her summer holidays with my family and her winters teaching school and tutoring the children of Rose and Joseph P. Kennedy. It was Doodie, as she became forever after, who sharpened my awareness to "the world around us" at the most sensitive and impressionable time of my childhood. She came to us when I was eight, my brother seven and sisters six and five.

Doodie was a cozy New Englander with keen blue inquisitive eyes and a face made beautiful through exposure to the elements that she so loved. She wore her hair in a French twist with tiny strands of it escaping into a fuzzy halo. We continually tried unsuccessfully to pat and tuck the "floating white" into shape. She wore it that way to the end of her life. Though she was truly oblivious to her appearance, her tastes were as firm as her sense of duty and ethics. She fancied Alice-blue and hand-wrought silver jewelry which she wore for special occasions. I thought, seeing her first through eight-year-old eyes, that she was middle-aged, though she was actually in her early thirties. She never seemed to change—even into her great age.

As she read us stories of our country's founding fathers, she seemed the very embodiment of the qualities that these pioneer democrats possessed. This gave reality to what she said and did, and impressed us greatly.

Because my father and mother were both nature lovers, we spent summers at our farm in the rolling hills of Kirtland, Ohio, where the Mormons stopped first on their westward trek to Utah. From the tenthouse in which we spent our first summers at the farm, we could view the slim, white spire of their Mormon Church of the Latter-Day Saints. It still punctuates that familiar view, surrounded by a sea of green trees dropping away to Lake Erie. In explaining the Mormon sect to us, Doodie made us aware that we were living in the midst of some of our country's history.

We spent those joyous summer days scrambling barefoot in the woods, over the meadows and into the deep ravine with its graveled rock floor which ran through our property. The arrowheads which my brother found added romance to our nights in the log cabin perched on one bank of the ravine. We swam in the "punch bowl," a natural pool carved by river and time. We caught crayfish on its banks and marveled at the profusion of wildlife, trees, rocks, ferns and flowers around us.

But it wasn't until Doodie came to us that we learned to identify each of the species. After her arrival birds weren't just birds. They were kildees, woodthrushes, downie woodpeckers, brown thrashers or meadow larks. Ferns weren't just feathery greens. They turned into Maidenhair, New York, Christmas and infinite others. It was Doodie who gave a name—Jewel Weed—to the delicate, dancing blossoms I loved so that carpeted the watery banks. My school essay on this exquisite flower and its habitat made its mark in the essay contest. Certain spiky "blue flowers," as we referred to them before Doodie's arrival, became the Great Lobelia. We used to follow Doodie deep into the woods to find the rare orchidaceous Moccasin Flower and the delicate-scented Trailing Arbutus. She would collect edible and inedible mushrooms and give them proper names; we soon learned to give a wide berth to the deadly varieties like Angel's Death Cup and Fly Aminita. The knowledge she imparted gave us the confidence to collect fearlessly the Campestra or field mushroom with its blushing pink underside, the dramatic pumpkin-colored Jack-o'-Lantern and the coral-like Oyster Mushroom. We loved writing messages and immortal verse and prose upon the white surface of the Polyporus, fan-shaped specimens that decorated tree stumps in the ravine.

When we first discovered the Tulip Tree growing tall and straight from the banks of our ravine, Doodie described its use for masts on ships. We collected its tulip-shaped leaves, pressing them into our tree books in which we recorded specimens as we found them.

We felt more kindly to the rain knowing that after it

was over Doodie would lead us "down to the chestnuts" in search of the incomparable Beefsteak mushrooms that grew on dead chestnut stumps. She showed us how to cook them in butter and lemon juice and serve them on toast. No caviar will ever seem more desirable.

We pored over books on birds, flowers, ferns, trees and mushrooms until we thought of ourselves as amateur naturalists. To this day I cherish notebooks in which I listed my first wild flowers, ferns, trees, birds and butterflies under Doodie's guidance during those thrilling days of discovery.

At Doodie's suggestion we planted and tended a vegetable garden, and we marketed its fruits to our parents, "to learn responsibilities and values" as Doodie put it.

Instead of hating to go to bed at night, with her guidance we managed to make it a beautiful ceremony. She took us out under the stars to identify the different constellations with such romantic mythological names as Venus, Mars, Cassiopeia's Chair or Orion's Belt. We would feel very small and full of awe, though strangely a part of all time and space as we watched with her the inexorable pacing of the stars. Because of Doodie, bedtime was no longer to be resented as a perfunctory close to a joyful day, but a romantic threshold to the miracle of night and its healing, refueling powers. She made it a time to savor the day's events.

Whenever we fell below the level of performance she had set for us, she would beguile us with irresistible tales of her prize and difficult pupils. There were the Kennedys, of course, who came high on her list. Once as a gentle rebuke I remember her saying, "Jack Kennedy studies hard. I feel sure that *he* will go far."

After many years away from home, I returned for a visit to my sister who lives near our farm. Doodie was living there too. I was stricken with hepatitis and as I lay recuperating, Doodie spent hours reading to me as she had in my childhood. One morning, just after she had closed the book, she was felled by a stroke which eventually was to take her life. It was characteristic that her last act was her pattern for each day, "doing for others."

She hath built an everlasting foundation with men
And she shall continue with their seed,

said Ecclesiastes in the Bible. One of the "seed," my niece Ann, wrote of Doodie:

"Doodie always loved the stars. We used to stand in the darkening forest waiting for the evening star to reach the gap in the trees. The quiet breathing of oncoming dusk and the pressure from her soft hand kept me waiting as silently as she. There was something exciting about standing next to Doodie on those evenings whispering about secret things and waiting. When the misty light of the stars would begin to appear over the rim of the trees, we would stop talking. Then there was just the rustle of the trees, Doodie's breathing, and the star to think about."

Doodie, or Miss Doolittle as I often called her, wore faded blue tennis shoes and V-necked blue dresses. Her hair was white and knotted in back. Little wisps often fell across her eyes. Her hands and face were covered with wrinkles, tiny ones that crisscrossed each other everywhere. The wrinkles were longer and pivoted about the corners of her eyes when she smiled, like the spokes of a wheel. There was one special wrinkle that stretched from her eye to her ear, and I had the secret feeling that it went inside her ear. Her hands were soft, and when I squeezed them it was like rubbing pie dough on a board. Little brown freckles from the sun covered her hands. I used to make up a game to see how many whole ones I could find between the wrinkles. Doodie was very brown and reminded me of a chipmunk balancing a white wig on his head. She even had a chipmunk way with her mouth.

It was not just Miss Doolittle's appearance, but the things she did as well, that intrigued me. She had some gray books. They were small and very worn and I can remember spending hours with them learning how to read. We sat outdoors because Doodie loved the outdoors. I learned the names of different ferns and flowers around us as their sounds fitted in with the ones we were studying in the gray books. Best of all, if I read a whole page with no mistakes she would let me look through her binoculars. Her binoculars were very precious, and I had to put the strap around my neck in case I dropped them.

Doodie knew the name of almost every bird, and nothing pleased her more than to find one she had never seen. We would wonder together what it could be, then Doodie would search through piles of bird books while I stood at her elbow staring intently at the pictures, sure I had found the unknown bird each time she turned the page. What fun when we found the right bird!

As I grew older, parties, school and friends occupied my time. I was no longer interested in the stars and the birds and the ferns. I was too busy in my own new world for Doodie's quiet ways. But she was never too busy for me. She knitted mittens, red and green ones, and as usual they were a size larger each birthday even though my hands had stopped growing.

The time came for me to go away to school. I went to say good-bye to Doodie one Sunday afternoon. A stillness came over me as I stopped in her doorway. She was sitting by the window, knitting and listening to a concert. Sunlight coming from the gap in the trees streamed in the window on her bent white head. In that quiet moment before she saw me, I saw Doodie for the first time with grown-up eyes. I only had time for a quick good-bye. That evening I flew to school, the red mittens Doodie had given me as a good-bye present in my suitcase. From my small window I watched the evening star rise and then disappear as we flew beneath it and away.

One Sunday in November I received a phone call. Doodie was dead.

At Christmas I went back to Doodie's room. Sunbeams were playing on her empty chair, reflecting off the radio, and dancing on the neatly stacked bird books. I looked out the window and remembered the lone star shining through the gap in the trees and the blinking red and green lights passing by the single star, then disappearing into the black night.

Wherever Doodie may be now—in some lovely woods, bird-watching or revealing the magic mysteries of the world of nature to some celestial first-grader, I hope she knows how firmly several generations of Halles bear her imprint. My sister Jane and her surgeon husband became professional naturalists and archeological skin divers, lecturing and showing films of their expeditions. My brother Walter and sister Margaret are ornithologists of considerable repute. My youngest sister Ann and her husband, both architects, live near our farm, recreating for their two boys what Doodie instilled in us. For me, Doodie developed an extra pair of eyes and a realization that some knowledge and intimacy with the natural world in its endless variety helps to keep our man-made world in its place.

※

THE TEACHER
AS PERSONALITY

Aaron Copland

THE TEACHER
AS PERSONALITY*

Aaron Copland

It is almost forty years since first I rang the bell at Nadia
Boulanger's Paris apartment and asked her to accept me
as her composition pupil. Any young musician may do
the same thing today, for Mademoiselle Boulanger lives
at the same address in the same apartment and teaches
with the same formidable energy. The only difference is
that she was then comparatively little known outside
the Paris music world, and today there are few musicians anywhere who would not concede her to be the
most famous of living composition teachers.

Our initial meeting had taken place in the Palace of
Fontainebleau several months before that first Paris visit.
Through the initiative of Walter Damrosch, a summer
music school for American students was established in a
wing of the Palace in 1921, and Nadia Boulanger was on
the staff as teacher of harmony. I arrived, fresh out of
Brooklyn, aged twenty, and all agog at the prospect of
studying composition in the country that had produced

* "The Teacher, Nadia Boulanger," copyright © 1960 by
Aaron Copland, from the book *Copland on Music*. Reprinted
by permission of Doubleday & Company, Inc.

Debussy and Ravel. A fellow student told me about Mademoiselle Boulanger and convinced me that a look-in on her harmony class would be worth my while. I needed convincing—after all, I had already completed my harmonic studies in New York and couldn't see how a harmony teacher would be of any help to me. What I had not foreseen was the power of Mademoiselle Boulanger's personality and the special glow that informs her every discussion of music, whether it be on the simplest or the most exalted plane.

The teaching of harmony is one thing; the teaching of advanced composition is something else again. The reason they differ so much is that harmonic procedures are deduced from known common practice, while free composition implies a subtle mixing of knowledge and instinct for the purpose of guiding the young composer toward a goal that can only be dimly perceived by both student and teacher. Béla Bartók used to claim that teaching composition was impossible to do well; he himself would have no truck with it. Mademoiselle Boulanger would undoubtedly agree that it is difficult to do well—and then go right on trying.

Actually Nadia Boulanger was quite aware that as a composition teacher she labored under two further dis-advantages: she was not herself a regularly-practicing composer and, in so far as she composed at all, she must of necessity be listed in that unenviable category of the woman composer. Everyone knows that the high achievement of women musicians as vocalists and instru-mentalists has no counterpart in the field of musical composition. This historically-poor showing has puzzled more than one observer. It is even more inexplicable when one considers the reputation of women novelists and poets, of painters and designers. Is it possible that there is a mysterious element in the nature of musical creativity that runs counter to the nature of the feminine mind? And yet there are more women composers than ever writing today; writing, moreover, music worth playing. The future may very well have a different tale to tell. For the present, however, no woman's name will be found on the list of world-famous composers.

To what extent Mademoiselle Boulanger had serious ambitions as composer has never been entirely established. She has published a few short pieces, and once told me that she had aided the pianist and composer Raoul Pugno in the orchestration of an opera of his. Mainly she was credited with the training of her gifted younger sister Lili, whose composing talent gained her the first Prix de Rome ever accorded a woman composer in more than a century of prize giving. It was an agonizing blow when Lili fell seriously ill and died in 1918 at the age of twenty-four. It was then that Nadia established the pattern of life that I found her living with her Russian-born mother in the Paris of the twenties.

Curiously enough I have no memory of discussing the role of women in music with Mademoiselle. Whatever her attitude may have been, she herself was clearly a phenomenon for which there was no precedent. In my own mind, she was a continuing link in that long tradition of the French intellectual woman in whose salon philosophy was expounded and political history made. In similar fashion, Nadia Boulanger had her own salon where musical aesthetics was argued and the musical future engendered. It was there that I saw, and sometimes even met, the musical great of Paris: Maurice Ravel, Igor Stravinsky, Albert Roussel, Darius Milhaud, Arthur Honegger, Francis Poulenc, Georges Auric. She was the friend of Paul Valéry and Paul Claudel, and liked to discuss the latest works of Thomas Mann, of Proust, and André Gide. Her intellectual interests and wide acquaintanceship among artists in all fields were an important stimulus to her American students; through these interests she whetted and broadened their cultural appetites.

It would be easy to sketch a portrait of Mademoiselle Boulanger as a personality in her own right. Those who meet her or hear her talk are unlikely to forget her physical presence. Of medium height and pleasant features, she gave off, even as a young woman, a kind of objective warmth. She had none of the ascetic intensity of a Martha Graham or the toughness of a Gertrude Stein. On the contrary, in those early days she possessed an almost old-fashioned womanliness—a womanliness that seemed quite unaware of its own charm. Her low-heeled shoes and long black skirts and pince-nez glasses contrasted strangely with her bright intelligence and lively temperament. In more recent years she has become smaller and thinner, quasi nun-like in appearance. But her low-pitched voice is as resonant as ever, and her manner has lost none of its decisiveness.

My purpose here, however, is to concentrate on her principal attribute, her gift as teacher. As her reputation spread, students came to her not only from America but also from Turkey, Poland, Chile, Japan, England, Norway and many other countries. How, I wonder, would each one of them describe what Mademoiselle's teachings gave him? How, indeed, does anyone describe adequately what is learned from a powerful teacher? I have never read a convincing account of the progress from student stage to that of creative maturity through a teacher's ministrations. And yet it happens: some kind of magic does indubitably rub off on the pupil. It begins, perhaps, with the conviction that one is in the presence of an exceptional musical mentality. By a process of osmosis, one soaks up attitudes, principles, reflections, knowledge. That last is a key word: It is literally exhilarating to be with a teacher for whom the art one loves has no secrets.

Nadia Boulanger knew everything there was to know about music; she knew the oldest and the latest music, pre-Bach and post-Stravinsky, and knew it cold. All technical know-how was at her fingertips: harmonic transposition, the figured bass, score reading, organ registration, instrumental techniques, structural analyses, the school fugue and the free fugue, the Greek modes and Gregorian chant. Needless to say, this list is far from exhaustive. She was particularly intrigued by new musical developments. I can still remember the eagerness of her curiosity concerning my jazz-derived rhythms of the early twenties, a corner of music that had somehow escaped her. Before long we were exploring polyrhythmic devices together—their cross-pulsations, their notation, and especially their difficulty of execution intrigued her. This was typical; nothing under the heading of music could possibly be thought of as foreign. I am not saying that she liked or even approved of all kinds of musical expression—far from it. But she had the teacher's consuming need to know how all music functions, skeletal frame of the harmony's progressive action. Her sense of contrast was acute; she was quick to detect longuers and any lack of balance. Her teaching, I suppose, was French in that she always stressed clarity of conception and elegance in proportion. It was her broadness of sympathy that made it possible for her to apply these general principles to the music of young men and women of so many different nationalities.

Many of these observations are based, of course, on experiences of a good many years ago. Much has happened to music since that time. The last decade, in particular, cannot have been an easy time for the teacher of composition, and especially for any teacher of the older generation. The youngest composers have taken to worshiping at strange shrines. Their attempt to find new constructive principles through the serialization of the chromatic scale has taken music in a direction for which Mademoiselle showed little sympathy in former years. The abandonment of tonality and the adoption of Webernian twelve-tone methods by many of the younger Frenchmen and even by Igor Stravinsky in his later years cannot have been a cause for rejoicing on the Rue Ballu. And yet, I have heard Mademoiselle Boulanger speak warmly of the music of the leader of the new movement, Pierre Boulez. Knowing the musician she is, I feel certain that she will find it possible to absorb the best of the newer ideas into her present-day thinking.

In the meantime, it must be a cause for profound satisfaction to Mademoiselle Boulanger that she has guided the musical destiny of so many gifted musicians: Igor Markevitch, Jean Francaix and Marcelle de Manziarly in France; Americans like Walter Piston, Virgil Thomson, Roy Harris, Marc Blitzstein, among the older men; Elliott Carter, David Diamond, Irving Fine, Harold Shapero, Arthur Berger among the middle generation, and youngsters like Easley Blackwood during the fifties.

In 1959, when Harvard University conferred an honorary degree on Nadia Boulanger, a modest gesture was made toward recognition of her standing as teacher and musician. America, unfortunately, has no reward commensurate with what Nadia Boulanger has contributed to our musical development. But, in the end, the only reward she would want is the one she already has: the deep affection of her many pupils everywhere.

✳

NEVER
TOO MANY
WOMEN

Isidor S. Ravdin

❈❈❈❈❈❈❈❈❈❈❈❈❈❈❈❈❈❈❈❈❈❈❈❈❈❈❈❈❈

Isidor S. Ravdin has held high offices in professional societies as well as high rank in the opinion of his fellows for a good third of a century. Professor of Surgery and Vice President in charge of medical affairs at the University of Pennsylvania for many years, he was also surgeon-in-chief at the University Hospital.

❈❈❈❈❈❈❈❈❈❈❈❈❈❈❈❈❈❈❈❈❈❈❈❈❈❈❈❈❈

⁜

NEVER
TOO MANY
WOMEN

Isidor S. Ravdin

The teacher who made the greatest impression on me as
a youngster was a teacher of history in the Evansville
(Indiana) High School. She was responsible for the
teaching of history. She knew it well and she taught it
superbly. There was never a dull moment when we
were with her.

While she was a stern disciplinarian in the conduct of
the class, she did it in such a way that no one realized
exactly what she was doing. It was not only how she
taught, but it was the remarkable personality of this
delightful woman. While devoted to the teaching of
history, she might just as well have been teaching English. When she found that one or more students were
interested in a particular aspect of history, she would
invite us to meet with her after hours. We came to love
history for history's sake. Most of us spent a good deal
of time after class reading various aspects of history that
were not assigned to us.

--⊰ *135* ⊱--

In those days Evansville was mostly an industrial city (a rather more important one than its size might indicate; its manufacturing capacity and situation on the Ohio River enabled it to develop during World War II the world's largest inland shipyards). The high school, because it was the only one in the city, then contained a broad cross-section of the city's youthful population. The student body was made up of about an even number of boys and girls; this fine teacher taught a good many school generations of them.

I kept in touch with her for some years after I left that school. Many were the letters that I received from her after her retirement, calling my attention to this article or that book or a specific lecture on some aspect of history that she thought might interest me. I am sure that I was not the only individual with whom she kept in contact. Her work was her life and she continued it until her death.

Last summer I went to Evansville for a class reunion. It had been a long time since I had seen many of my classmates. Although their names were familiar their faces were not. In discussing teachers with a number of them, I think it was nearly unanimous that Abigail (oddly enough, we all at this time referred to her affectionately by her first name) strongly influenced many members of the class.

Perhaps we remembered her with gratitude because she succeeded in broadening our intellectual horizons, guiding and stimulating our interests in directions which we might have disregarded with another teacher or never have even known existed.

A good many years ago, when my wife and I were in

Edinburgh, we had the opportunity of having dinner with a Nobel laureate from Germany. He had been in this country for a year or two at one of our great eastern universities. He even considered accepting the offer of a Chair at that institution. He said that he turned it down because "you have too many women teaching in American primary schools." Later he came to this country with his family when it became impossible for him to live in Germany. We talked about that statement he had made to us some years previously. I then told him the story I have told here, and I hope it made some impression on him. I feel sure it did. We need more teachers like Abigail, well-trained and devoted to their effort.

＊

REVELATION
FOR A
TEEN-AGER

Cornelia Otis Skinner

Stage star, writer, producer and monologist, Cornelia Otis Skinner can look back at a lot of teachers she encountered at Bryn Mawr, the Sorbonne and two French schools of the theater in addition to her elementary and secondary education. The versatility of this famous personality was phenomenal; in the theater she played in everything from Tweedles *to* Candida.

REVELATION
FOR A
TEEN-AGER

Cornelia Otis Skinner

As I look back on the years of my somewhat sketchy education (I did graduate from school, but went only part way through college), I recall several teachers as well as one or two professors to whom I owe life-long debts of gratitude for having inspirited my days of study.

However, there was one teacher in particular whose influence on me was not *merely* inspiriting, it was *downright* inspiriting. This was Miss Augusta Choate, my English teacher at the Baldwin School in Bryn Mawr, Pennsylvania.

I must preface my tribute to this wonderful lady by confessing that up until the time I came under her academic spell when I was about fifteen, I was a dreadful student. As a matter of truth, I was a rather dreadful little girl and an even more dreadful teen-ager. I shared the popular point of view of the other dreadful little girls and teen-agers that school counted only during recess hours, that lessons were a bore to be endured through yawning, smothering giggles and writing Yale, Harvard or Princeton Rah-Rah! in the margins of text-books, and that any classmate who applied herself seriously to study was a "greasy grind" and socially taboo. My monthly report card brought tears to my mother, glum silence from my father (he hadn't been a very good scholar himself), and from myself promises of reformation which the next week went the way of all such promises. In mathematics I was a dunce (and still am); I got through French only because I could speak it and through Caesar's *Gallic War* only by using a trot (a misdemeanor for which I could have been expelled). I enlivened my junior biology class by throwing up the day we dissected a frog, and although outside of school I had always been an avid reader with a preference for Zane Grey and Elinor Glynn, any required reading for English was in the nature of a painful chore.

Then one day the clouds parted and the light shone and I can still remember with a thrill the very moment. It happened in English class. Miss Choate was talking about Addison and Steele, giving examples of their style by reading aloud certain excerpts from the *Roger de Coverly* papers of the *Spectator*. She read and talked with wit and the quietly affectionate enthusiasm of the profound scholar who delights in sharing her intellectual treasure with her listeners. All at once a strange excitement began to stir in my footling teen-age brain; English prose began to take on appealing shape and the 18th Century began to come alive. I found myself murmuring aloud "Why this is fun! This is actual fun! In fact, it's glorious fun!" The realization was in the nature of a revelation. I'm certain Miss Choate was aware of my awakening. She asked me to stay for a moment after class, and I sat down before her desk in a sort of state of blissful grace listening avidly while she talked further and marked certain passages in my textbook which she said might amuse me.

From that moment on English became my favorite subject. I used to linger after class nearly every day to ask Miss Choate questions about prose and poetry . . . about the Romantics, the Georgians, the Elizabethans . . . even Chaucer! I drank in avidly every word she told me, and I think she was happy that I wanted to know. My marks in the subject began to soar . . . even my other grades went up . . . all, that is, except math. When at long last I took my Bryn Mawr entrance exams, I received one of the highest marks ever given out for English literature. (I also received the lowest algebra mark in the college's history.)

Miss Choate left Baldwin and opened her own school in Boston. This gentle, scholarly, wise woman died a few years ago. Her memory lives on in the minds and hearts of the pupils who learned from her and who loved her. But in none is her memory cherished with more gratitude than in mine.

※

AN
ARTIST'S
MEMORIES

Thomas Hart Benton

One of the towering figures in American art for the last half century, Thomas Hart Benton comes from a family eminent in the history of Missouri—he bears the name of his great-uncle, a founder of Jacksonian democracy. His murals are fittingly placed in the State Capitol and the Truman Library in Independence, among other buildings. He has been a professional painter since 1912, after a teacher in the Western Military Academy helped him discover what an artist's life might be.

‍*

AN
ARTIST'S
MEMORIES

Thomas Hart Benton

So many people have put stimulating ideas into my head, and these, of course, are the real teachers, that I can hardly number them. Furthermore, it is hard to dig out of a nearly forgotten past and put into words the meaning they gave to life, especially in one's earlier years.

Morris Ernst himself has his place among my later teachers, along with such of his friends as Jerome Frank, Caroline Pratt, Charles Beard, Alvin Johnson, Roger Baldwin, John Dewey. And there are plenty of others: the daily companions of my youth, competitors in my trade, my wife, my students.

However, I believe the teacher who made what is perhaps the most decisive impression in my life, the one which occasioned a most decisive turn therein, was a portly, white-haired, oldish lady who caught me in my seventeenth year when I was putting in a sojourn at a military academy at Alton, Illinois. (This would have been in 1906.)

She was head of the English department at that place and she undertook to relieve my general restlessness and boredom with the military business, and related subjects, by introducing me to English poetry. She took me on not only in her regular classes, but after school hours and at suppers in her home in the town, where she coaxed me into reading out loud from Wordsworth, Shelley, Keats, Rossetti and other poets most popular at the time. It was different, or anyway seemed different, from the poetry we had read in the library at home—anthologies mostly. I already had absorbed considerable of Byron and Poe, and of course there was the *Rubaiyat of Omar Khayyam* which was standard adolescent literature in my time. I also knew a lot of poetic stuff like the mythologies of Greece, Rome and the North countries, the *Arabian Nights* and of course the Bible. After all, I came out of a talking, arguing family. You had to read to hold your own. So I'd read quite a lot, but never with the precision the old lady demanded.

Furthermore, Robert Browning was her special love, and it was through Browning's poems about Italian painters and her romantic enthusiasm for these that she made her impact on me. She exalted my ego, a young artist's budding ego perhaps. Maybe her special interest in me came from my knack for drawing, already *pretty* well developed by then in spite of my lack of training, which made me a part of her dream world, the world of Browning's Fra Lippo Lippi, Andrea del Sarto, etc. She took me on, as I said, because I was bored and restless, and being a good old lady she felt sorry for me.

I don't think she affected any of my classmates as she did me. But then she knew that I was considerably more experienced about life than the run of boys in the school. I'd lived in Washington when my father was a member of Congress, had worked with a survey team in the southwest mining areas of Missouri and Oklahoma, even acted professionally for a while as a newspaper cartoonist on the *American* in the rough mining city of Joplin, Missouri, with the kind of adventures that involved. What thoughts I gave to a picture-making career led to the newspaper world, to a resumption of cartooning. Of that I wrote in the first chapter of *An Artist in America:*

"I learned the jargon of the press and inked my drawings under the red hot corrugated iron roof of the office. It was my business to draw some prominent person of the town each day. The heads of my drawings I made big and set them on little bodies, according to the cartoon fashion of the day. Around my people I drew the paraphernalia of their trade or business. Someone in the office supplied the comment. This was a feature designed to interest the town in the new paper. How I did the work is a mystery to me. How I made the heads recognizable as individuals is beyond explanation. I would start with the nose and hang the other features on it, but somehow or other, in this crazy way, I managed to make likenesses.

"All summer I worked for the *American*. In the afternoons I clamped my foot importantly on the bar rail of the House of Lords and drank beer with the miners, the mine owners, the businessmen and the newspapermen. Everything was jake. I was a man—and free.

I was completely satisfied, except when I caught sight of my face in the mirror of the bar. It annoyed me that I looked so young. . . .

"One day toward autumn I went home for a week and my family were very uneasy about my staying in Joplin. They were not sure but that the town offered too many opportunities for a seventeen-year-old boy to go to hell. Besides, they were worried about my education. They wanted me to finish high school and go to college. Having tasted freedom, academic harness was abhorrent to me, and I balked. What! Another year of high school and then four years more? Unthinkable. I was a man of the world, and no damned schoolboy. If I quit the paper, I wanted to go to Chicago and study art. I knew there was a big art school in Chicago. I'd study there for a year and then get a big-time newspaper job and get rich. The family objected to this and after hours of discussion we reached a compromise. I agreed to do a year in a military school up in Alton, Illinois, if I could go to Chicago the next. I gave up my job on the Joplin *American* and found myself strutting in a gray uniform. I couldn't smoke in the military academy so I chewed tobacco. I went out for the football team and got my letter. When the football season ended the place was a bore to me. I couldn't stand it."

That was when my Browning-inspired teacher revealed a very different prospect than the newspaper career I had envisaged. It opened up toward a world of serious painting, the study of nature, and emphasized the great values of a life of art. It set up in me the first definite urge toward these that I remember.

At seventeen I may have been, surely was, spiritually

and intellectually innocent but not physically so. I know that youngsters are supposed to fall in love with older women under these circumstances, but it was not so here. While I was at the military school I had a girl with whom I corresponded regularly. She was but slightly older than I and was not portly. Maybe I was susceptible to poetry because of her absence.

Of course I never did tell my teacher what she had done for me or thank her for it. Unfortunately youth has no time for such niceties. When I left the school I went to Chicago and got so involved in the studies of art I took up there I just forgot her. After that I went to Paris. I did keep up the poetry reading, French as well as English, for ten or twelve years, so I did have her in the back of my mind. But I never wrote her—she would not have understood my new jargon anyway. Too bad, but that's the way it is.

For all her enthusiasms, sympathies and intuitions, she would not have had any very clear notions of what an actual life of art might be. Her experiences would not have given her much insight. But she had an idea. More than an idea. She had a passionate conviction that it was a fine kind of life, a superior kind, a life worth striving for.

She was right.

I've lived that life and I've often thought of my debt to that poetry-reading old lady who first encouraged me to do so.

✳

DISCOVERING PHILOSOPHY

Tess Helburn

Housewife and mother of two sons is the way Tess Helburn describes herself, but she also taught freshman history for half a dozen years and coordinated and led the outdoor living program of the Peace Corps Training Unit at Montana State University. She is now Chairman of the Montana Indian Committee of the American Friends Service Committee and a member of the Friends Regional Executive Board.

DISCOVERING
PHILOSOPHY

Tess Helburn

I came to the University of Chicago in the middle 1930's from a medium-sized, somewhat better than average Iowa high school in which I had done rather well. In those days, and surely still, there were many great men and many good teachers on the faculty. Before getting to the University the student knew some of the famous names. During freshman week several others were impressed upon the poor newcomer as "must" professors from whom to take a class.

In my time we were required to take five survey courses in which the best-known professors each taught his own specialty to beginners. Some of these men were good teachers; others should have stayed with their graduate students in their laboratories. Each survey also involved one discussion a week, and for a leader in this discussion you might get an unknown who was truly an inspired teacher or you might get the best geneticist on the staff "discussing" beginning biology so that it was utterly incomprehensible. You were stuck with your leader though you were permitted to attend other discussion classes. Attending second discussions became common practice, so that good teacher-leaders had students sitting on radiators and hanging out the windows.

Thanks to this system I attended classes taught by ever so many men whom I remember as stimulating, provocative, warm, helpful, exciting. They were in all fields at all levels of my studies. I had three years of the Hutchins-Adler "Great Books" course. I hung in the window to hear the philosopher Morris Cohen when he first came to Chicago. I rang doorbells to help get T. V. Smith into the State Senate as an auxiliary to his philosophy lectures. I campaigned after his economics classes for former United States Senator Paul Douglas; got basic social studies from a former social worker, Louis Wirth, and a future college president, Harry Gideonse; and biology from the Swedish-born physiologist, A. J. Carlson; sat fascinated by Ferdinand Schevill's presentations on art, and subjected myself to amusing and cutting commentaries from Jane Addams's brilliant nephew "Teddy" Linn on English compositions. It was an exhilarating time and place.

However, it was one of the not-quite-so-great men but utterly-beyond-description teachers who made me better able to appreciate all the others, and made it possible for me to gain at least a bit of what they were so devotedly trying to teach me. And I can't even remember, for certain, his full name. Everyone called him "Doc" and the rest was Osborn. My introduction to him was a by-product of the University's system of that day.

When I enrolled I thought I knew what I wanted to do. I'd decided as early as freshman week, when all the ropes were explained to us, that I would "challenge" as many of the requirements as I could and thus have more time for my chosen fields. The process of challenging was very simple. You just went to the proper office, registered to take the examination in the course next time it was given, paid the fee, got a ticket admitting you to the exam and then watched for announcements of the time it was to be given. If you passed you were spared taking the course. This I did in a couple of courses early my freshman year. But I also decided I had enough background to do it in the Humanities Survey if I waited until spring to take the exam and in the meantime attended lectures on phases of the subject about which I was hazy or knew nothing—philosophy for one. My roommate was registered for the course at one of my free hours, so I could attend with her.

That first Humanities lecture, during the second week after the Fall quarter began, turned out to be the beginning of a change in my college curriculum and what college meant to me, although I didn't know it at the time. The lectures were held in the Gothic theater, which seated about seven hundred people. Somewhere in the vicinity of four hundred students were registered for the course. A rather smallish man was standing on the constructed platform in front of the stage. He was dressed in gray with a very big gold watch chain and Phi Beta Kappa key across his vest. He took off his watch, chain and key and placed them on the lectern, waited for the bell—and then preached to us. Before he had preached ten minutes, it was quieter than any church in which I have been. I think he talked about early Greek philosophers. His listeners were utterly entranced.

Soon I found that I was attending these Humanities lectures more regularly than some of the courses for which I was formally registered. For all the remarkable men on the humanities faculty, he is the one who stands out in memory, and I don't think I am alone in that feeling. Before the first quarter was half over, there would be up to seven hundred people streaming in to hear him—and one came early not to have to sit in the balcony. It was a real breach of etiquette to sneeze or drop a pencil while he was preaching—and no one did. You put all your books and extras under your seat before class, held your notebook firmly on your lap and prayed you wouldn't run out of ink—no ball-points in those days.

Then in the silence he preached and preached about philosophers and philosophy and ideas. To seven hundred kids who didn't know a rationalist from a dualist, had never heard of an empiricist or nominalist or materialist, philosophy became something alive, exciting, worth sitting up all night and arguing about in the dorm while the unfortunates who didn't have the course played bridge.

Since I was not registered for it, I had no assigned discussion section, so I asked to attend Doc's. He was almost as much fun and as fascinating while discussing the *Song of Roland*, the fall of the Roman Empire or the structure of Gothic cathedrals as he was with his own philosophy. Before the year was over, or I had actually taken that Humanities exam, I transferred my minor from language to philosophy. I have had so much enjoyment from Philosophy ever since that first lecture, it wouldn't have mattered that I could never have earned my living at it.

I had some fringe benefits from the stimulation and excitement of Doc's lectures. I could never have gotten by the required math courses had it not been for the girl next door to me in the dorm, a fine math major who was as much at sea about philosophy as I was about math. After we got through cramming each other for our exams, I didn't miss a math problem and she didn't do at all badly in philosophy.

More years later than I will admit, I taught a general course at the college level, and whenever I came to the philosophy part of it I relaxed with confidence. The great names at Chicago probably could not have done this for me, but Doc Osborn was always in front of me as I attempted to intrigue freshmen with philosophic ideas—with what success I am uncertain.

Having rather handily passed the Humanities Survey, I had a course in general philosophy of which Doc taught the first quarter and all the rest of the year conducted once-a-week "help" sessions which I attended religiously although they were held at some such ghastly hour of the day as 4 P.M. I didn't miss one, although I did miss many dinners as Doc stood around after the sessions with ten or twelve of us and enlightened us endlessly. His help at these sessions was so strong that it really didn't matter that I could play at helping T. V. Smith fail to get elected Congressman-at-

Large instead of paying attention to his course on modern philosophy, because Doc could be counted on to fill any gaps.

Considering how much his courses meant to us, how interested I and many others became in philosophy because of him, it is surprising how little we really knew about him and how little personal contact we had with him outside the teaching relationship. I do remember with some real pride that he called me up at the dorm shortly before the final examination to ask if I were having any problems or whether he could help me. Yes, he could. I went to his cubbyhole of an office and for a couple of hours received lucid, logical answers to everything that was bothering me from Zeno to Hegel.

The only other contact I had with him could be called social—faculty night at a girl's dorm. Maybe my contemporaries remember. You invited two or three faculty couples for dinner at the dorm, and you "entertained" them. Weeks before the excruciating event a paper was put on the bulletin board and the girls signed for the faculty members they wanted to invite. The three most popular received invitations to dinner and an evening. Each faculty member was assigned to a table; no student was to monopolize a guest, but no guest was to be left standing alone or untalked to for a second.

Doc was always on the list, and three times in my two years in the dorm he was invited, although invitations had to be spread around some. It was forced and stilted, and as I look back it must have been as appalling for the guests as for the girls—probably much more so since we could be a bit moon-eyed and they obviously could not. Be that as it may, on all three occasions I made it through the crush at one time or another in the evening to talk to Doc.

Even so, I don't know much about him personally. He wasn't very prepossessing, a slim, straight person, certainly no more than five feet eight inches. I suppose the novelist's term "hawk-faced" would be close to an apt description of his looks. He was just more than a bit gray; his slightly receding hair was going gray, his eyes were gray, his very proper suits with vests were always gray. He was a bachelor.

There were lots of stories about him, any of which, or none of which, might have been true. No one that I knew ever bothered or had the nerve to verify any, although we believed them all. He was a Ph.D. in philosophy, but it was said he was a Doctor of Divinity also and previously. Very believable from the way he preached philosophy, and also from what he gave us of comparative religion on the side. It was also said he had been a chaplain—or was it member of an ambulance unit?—during World War I. He must have been well under forty when I first had him as a teacher.

The year I was a junior Doc left Chicago to become head of the department of philosophy at Lawrence, Kansas, a place that seemed the end of the earth to me at the time. I remember I was desolate, but not enough to write him. I did compose several letters to him in my thoughts, but whenever I was free of term papers, exciting classes, dull library work or preparing for tests it seemed there were hundreds of things which needed doing, and letters just didn't get put on paper.

So there is no way he could ever know that I couldn't have enjoyed or appreciated the faculty greats or been so happy preparing for my degree if it hadn't been for him. But for him, I'd have continued fighting languages with little success and less love. I would have missed out on the greatest fun I had in college, the dorm bull sessions and late afternoon discussions in a wholly new field which he opened to us. I could never have tried so enthusiastically to teach in my own beginning college course what ideas are and about some of the people who had them.

I have, year in and year out, had him in front of me as I faced seventy or eighty (not seven hundred) students who have never heard of empiricism, rationalism, Plato or Hegel and tried to make their meanings and ideas come alive. I can't preach, and I don't recommend it for those who can't do it naturally, and you could never hear a pin drop in my classes. I'm certain I can't make it so logical you can't miss it and have to get all excited about it, but I wouldn't have given such a course more than a frightened passing nod if it hadn't been for Doc's teaching.

I rather hope Doc Osborn never sees this, yet I wonder whether he will otherwise ever realize what he opened to us and what fun we had with the world he opened. I don't know where he is now. But it doesn't matter too much, for he still lives in my still very juvenile excitement with ideas which he made more than academic twiddle-twaddle or indigestible quibbling. I only hope that in my teaching I have excited one person in something half as much as he excited me; that I have made just one thing as much fun for one person as he made philosophy for me.

☀

DEAR
MISS O'NEILL

Leo Rosten

****

This author, a special consultant to Look *magazine, is as well known under his pseudonym, Leonard Q. Ross, as under his own name, Leo Rosten. He has been that unusual combination, a humorist who can also write serious fiction, turn to non-fiction and in between carve out a career as a political scientist and adviser to government agencies. His contribution, originally written for this book, first appeared in* Look.

****

DEAR
MISS O'NEILL

Leo Rosten

On the hellish hot days (and the only city more hellish than Chicago, where this happened, is Bombay), Miss O'Neill would lift her wig and gently scratch her pate. She did it absently, without interrupting whatever she was saying or doing.

We always watched this with fascination. Miss O'Neill was our seventh-grade teacher, and it was the consensus of my more sophisticated peers that Miss O'Neill had, until very recently, been a nun. That was the only way they could explain the phenomenon of her baldness. Miss O'Neill, they whispered, had left her holy order for heartrending reasons, and the punishment her superiors had decreed was that she become a slave in the George Howland Elementary School on Sixteenth Street.

We never knew Miss O'Neill's first name (teachers never had a first name), and when my mother once asked me how old she was, I answered, "Oh, she's *old*."

All teachers are *old*. And old means at least thirty, even forty—which, to an eleven-year-old, is as decrepit and remote and meaningless as, say, sixty or seventy, though not one hundred.

Miss O'Neill was dumpy, moonfaced, sallow-skinned, colorless, and we loathed her as only a pack of West Side barbarians could loathe a teacher of arithmetic. She did not teach arithmetic—but that is how much all of us hated her.

She was our English teacher, a 33rd-degree perfectionist who drilled us endlessly, mercilessly, in spelling and grammar and diction and syntax. She had a hawk's eye for a dangling participle or an upright non sequitur, a "not *quite* right" word or a fruity solecism. (Did you know that "solecism" comes from the contempt of the Greek patricians for the dialect that thrived in Soloi?) Whenever any of us made an error in composition *or* recitation, Miss O'Neill would send the culprit to the blackboard to "diagram" the sentence! That was the torture we most resented.

We had to designate the function of every word and phrase and clause; we had to describe how each part of every sentence worked; we had to explain how the parts fit together, and how they mesh and move to wheel out meaning. Before our whole runnynosed congregation, an innocent child had himself or herself to locate an error, identify a malfunction, explain the *reason* for the correction Miss O'Neill impassively awaited. She waited as if she could sit there until Gabriel blew his kazoo, as our devastating humor had it. And if the offered correction was itself wrong, Miss O'Neill compounded the discipline by making the errant urchin diagram *that* on the board, instructing him to persevere.

Some kids would break into a sweat as they floundered around, failing to hit the bull's eye, praying that Miss O'Neill would end their agony by the generous gift of one good and true answer. But that Miss O'Neill rarely proffered. Instead, she would turn her inquisition from the pupil at the blackboard to the helots in the chairs. "Well, class? . . . Jacob, do *you* know the answer? . . . No? . . . Shirley? . . . Harold? . . . Joseph?" So heartless and unyielding was her method.

Each day, as we poured out of George Howland like Cheyennes en route to a scalping, we would pause briefly to pool our misery and voice our rage over the fate that had condemned us to such an abecedarian. Had we known Shakespeare, we would have added one word to Hamlet's brutal advice to Ophelia, making it, with feeling, "Get thee back to a nunnery."

Miss O'Neill never raised her voice, never lost her patience, never got angry. What was even more surprising, she never had to punish or even threaten our most ingenious troublemakers. For some reason we never discovered, the small impertinences and sly infractions and simulated incomprehensions with which we shrewdly persecuted our other teachers never seemed to get anywhere in the tight, shipshape world of Miss O'Neill's classroom.

I say that my comrades and I hated Miss O'Neill— but that is not entirely true. I only pretended to hate her. In our sidewalk conclaves, when we chortled over the latest tour de force of Douglas Fairbanks, or

mourned the defeat of the noble Cubs by the disgusting
White Sox, or matched extravagances about what we
would do if we found *ten million dollars,* or imagined
the possible surrender of one or another maiden to our
lascivious fumblings, I, too, would howl about Miss
O'Neill's tyranny, cursing her adamantine ways as fer-
vently as any of my companions. So strong is the desire
of a boy to "belong," to be no different from even the
grubbiest of his fellows.

But secretly my respect for Miss O'Neil—nay, my
affection—increased week by week. For I was exhila-
rated by what I can only call the incorruptibility of her
instruction. I found stirring within myself a sense of
excitement, of discovery, a curious quickening of the
spirit that attends initiation into a new world. Though I
could not explain it in these words, and would have
scorned the Goody-Two-Shoes overtone, I felt that
Miss O'Neill was leading me not through the irksome
labyrinth of English but into a sunlit realm of order and
meaning. Her iron rules, her crisp strictures, her con-
stant corrections were not, to me, the irritating nit-
picking they were to my buddies. They were sudden
flashes of light, glimpses of the magic hidden within
prose, intoxicating visions of that universe that awaits
understanding. It was as if a cloak of wonder had been
wrapped around the barren bones of grammar. For it
was not grammar or diction or syntax that Miss O'Neill,
whether she knew it or not, was introducing me to. She
was revealing language as the beautiful beat and life of
logic. She was teaching what earlier generations so beau-
tifully called "right reason."

The most astonishing thing about Miss O'Neill was

that she proceeded on the sanguine assumption that she could actually teach a pack of potential roller-skate-derby fans how to write clear, clean, correct sentences, organized in clear, clean, correct paragraphs—in their native tongue.

I do not think Miss O'Neill had the slightest aware-ness of her hold and influence on me. Nor was she especially interested in me. She never betrayed an ink-ling of preference or favoritism for any of her captive flock. Nor was she interested in the high, immortal reaches of the language whose terrain she so briskly charted. She was a technician, pure and simple—effi-cient, conscientious, immune to the malarkey some pupils resorted to. Nothing derailed Miss O'Neill from professionalism.

And that is the point. Miss O'Neill did not try to please us. She did not even try to like us. She certainly made no effort to make us like her. She valued results more than affection, and respect more than popularity. Not endowed with loving or lovable qualities, she did not bother regretting it, or denying it, or trying to compensate for it. She went about her task with no concessions to the we're-all-friends or think-of-me-as-your-pal gambits. She used the forthright "I want" or "You go" instead of the repulsive "Shall we?" Alien to humor or affection, she concentrated on nothing more than the transmission of her knowledge and her skill.

I think Miss O'Neill knew what the evangelists of "progressive" education are bound to rediscover: that the young prefer competence to "personality" in a teacher, and certainly to camaraderie; that a teacher need be neither an ogre nor a confidant; that what is hard to master gives children special rewards (pride, self-respect, the gratification of succeeding) precisely because difficulties have been conquered; that there may indeed be no easy road to learning some things, and no "fascinating" or "fun" way of learning some things really well.

I do not know whether Miss O'Neill infected anyone else in my seventh grade with a passion for, or even an abiding interest in, English. To me, she was a force of enlightenment.

She has long since shucked her travail among the West Side aborigines. Perhaps she has departed this baffling world to don wings—and, I hope, golden locks, to replace that wig under whose gauzy base she scratched relief from itching. If she is still alive, she must be in her dotage. And if she is among us still, I hope she somehow gets word of these long-belated thanks for a job supremely well done. I have never forgotten what she taught.

To this day, whether I am wrestling an intransigent sentence, or stand glazed before a buck-passing phrase whose improvement eludes me, or flagellate myself for some inspiration that might light up the drab texture of tired prose, whether I am winded by a rodomontade clause in Shaw or knocked cold by a tortured sentence in Talcott Parsons, I find myself thinking of Miss (What-oh-what?) O'Neill—and, sighing, take a sheet of paper and diagram the English until I know—and know *why*—it is right or wrong, or how it can be swept clean of that muddleheadedness that plagues us all.

※

THE
ROAD TO
SAMARKAND

Isabelle K. Savell

❋❋❋❋❋❋❋❋❋❋❋❋❋❋❋❋❋❋❋❋❋❋❋❋❋❋❋❋❋❋

A newspaperwoman (one of the organizers of the New York Newspaper Guild), magazine writer and biographer of Emily Eaton Hepburn, Daughter of Vermont, *Mrs. Savell held important government posts in Washington and New York, most recently as Administrative Assistant to Governor Nelson A. Rockefeller, before her appointment in 1965 as a member of her State's Workmen's Compensation Board.*

❋❋❋❋❋❋❋❋❋❋❋❋❋❋❋❋❋❋❋❋❋❋❋❋❋❋❋❋❋❋

THE
ROAD TO
SAMARKAND

Isabelle K. Savell

I've stalled a bit on answering your letter (suggesting I write about a favorite teacher). My first reaction to it was: "But of course, no." Unfortunately, perhaps, I didn't get that response written because I kept thinking of the teachers who were important to me, whose hands and guidance I can still feel, almost palpably, and I thought I owed it to them and to myself to set down some of these ruminations on paper, for better or for worse.

This is not a wholly disinterested thought. I was myself a teacher at one time: journalism at Sarah Lawrence College in Bronxville, N.Y. And at the end of that interlude I worked with the President of the college on a book called *A New Design for Women's Education*. I also have a son who is studying to be a teacher—of languages—for the self-propelled reason that, as he put it:

"Perhaps, perhaps, if people understood each other better, the world would not be in such a mess."

(I know: people can still create a mess in the same language, but still, he has a point.)

Perhaps the most impelling reason why I wanted to set down some of these thoughts, however, was because of my mother, who was also a teacher. The best I've ever known, although I never sat in her class. She is a vital part of my recollection of those in whose classes I did sit because, thanks to her, I was able to profit from or at least recognize a good teacher when I saw one.

Mother was a sunbonnet-pioneer type—we forget how the rush of events has telescoped our history. Before her marriage she taught in a country school on the plains of Colorado, living with the parents of some of her students.

After her marriage she "proved up" on a dry ranch near the Greenhorn range in southern Colorado, while my father worked in the iron-and-steel town 25 miles away. There was no school on the plains, but as the range was fenced and ranch families began to grow, the ranchers appealed to Mother to start one. She did. She helped them build a one-room log schoolhouse with long tables and hard wooden benches and a pot-bellied stove, and she taught all eight grades there. Some of her students were bigger than she was, but she was a tough disciplinarian and they respected her. Most of them walked for miles across the prairies to reach the school, and they were glad enough to be there.

I was still too young to attend, but on rare occasions —and they *were* rare for me—she would let me climb into the spring wagon and drive with her and my brothers to the schoolhouse and stay the day. I can still see her sitting ramrod straight on the wagon seat in shirtwaist and skirt and sailor hat, her face heavily creamed against the burning sun, prodding the jogging horse to move faster across the hard, dry plain.

She kept a set of McGuffey's *Readers* over the door at home, and used them, but what she mostly taught or communicated, I think, was a sense of horizons with limitless challenges and demands for the human spirit, and the awareness that time is short. That, plus a quenchless curiosity.

Her world was circumscribed by the horizons of the plains on which she spent her life; but her grandparents had crossed the Atlantic in a sailing ship, and gone on across the plains in a covered wagon, and she inherited their drive and endurance and vision, and was as much a citizen of her universe as the space traveler of today. Lucky me!

Eventually, as we grew, the ranch was sold (to an Iowa schoolteacher), and we children attended school in the town of Pueblo. There, when I reached high school, something sensational happened to me: a teacher who scared the wits out of me and galvanized my thinking. Harriette Hill's subject was dramatics, but her country was the world. She had a finely chiseled nose which quivered a bit when she was angry, flashing gray-green eyes, a firm mouth and jaw, and she wore her hair in a pompadour. What scared me was that she demanded everything from us, thus fulfilling the Emersonian observation that our greatest need is for someone who will make us do what we *can*.

Her students—25 or 30 of us in a class—were the meager fruit of the prairies and a steel town. But she limned and peopled a whole new world for us, a creative, glowing, questing, questioning, demanding world. We read plays, produced them, discussed them, mounted them; we studied the careers of actors and actresses and playwrights. In addition to Shakespeare and Molière she introduced us to the New York of Heywood Broun and Alexander Woollcott; she made us read everything we could find about some rising new stars on Broadway named Lunt and Fontanne, and a promising young ingenue named Hayes, Helen—then playing together in *Clarence*. She alerted us to that then-dawning genius of Eugene O'Neill, still known chiefly for his one-act plays but soon to produce *Emperor Jones* and *Strange Interlude*. She made the Provincetown Players, George Cram Cook, Susan Glaspell and that whole creative group, including Edna St. Vincent Millay, a vital part of our lives.

I always assumed that Harriette Hill came straight to us from New York, and indeed her familiarity with the theater and its satellite activities—the Brouns, Mantles, Nathans and so on—makes that seem likely, but at the time I did not probe. What was important was that she was a tyrant in long skirts, eternally dissatisfied with us, eternally demanding the impossible, and somehow, miraculously, making us produce and deliver far beyond what we thought we could do. Years later, I remember, she visited me, and I, both proud and tense as a violin string, was shocked when she said:

"It's about time you called me Harriette."

I had never dreamed of doing such a thing, and it took some doing even after she suggested it. Such was her impact that I cannot imagine that any of her pupils were ever quite the same once they had studied and worked with her. I know my brother was as impressed and galvanized by her as I was. Indeed, I recall that when a traveling stock company came to the Grand Opera House once in something like *Chu Chin Chow*, my brother, recently home from college, invited Harriette with a great flourish to attend, and he acquired and wore top hat and tails for the occasion. I doubt that there were any top hats then in the whole of Pueblo except for those of the Elks.

I studied too under some excellent teachers at the University of Colorado, but the two I remember best were a husband-and-wife team in English literature who, with great learning, insight and kinetic joy of communication, enriched the lives of all of us who had a chance to study with them. No one who ever sat in their classes left without a new, vibrant fourth-dimensional understanding of his world.

In my salad days as a reporter on *The Brooklyn Eagle*, I covered from time to time the Brooklyn Institute of Arts and Sciences, a kind of latter-day Chautauqua, at the Academy of Music. Once, I recall, I heard a lecturer there named Dallas Lore Sharp talk about education. He said he had gone to school for twenty years but had gotten his education in four days. Those were the intensely significant days when a teacher had zeroed in on something in his own life and kindled a light that would illuminate his path for decades to come. "Don't *tell* us about the lady-slipper you saw on your way to school; go *get* it and bring it to class; we're studying botany today." That sort of thing.

I was thinking about that recently in connection with the husband-and-wife team, Professor and Mrs. George

F. Reynolds. We used to argue on the campus about which was the greater teacher, but it was a futile argument. Both had a profound influence on all of us; they were the mind-expanders of that time and place, summoning the great and colorful figures of literature to be our companions.

In an era when the chief symbols of our world were Calvin Coolidge and the Charleston, Mrs. Reynolds was re-creating for us—there on a Rocky Mountain college campus—the anguish and yearnings of James Elroy Flecker's Persian confectioner, Hassan, who in the end abandoned his shop in Baghdad and took the golden road to Samarkand. Such a spell did she weave, such a hold did she have, that today, this summer, forty years later, I am setting forth to take the golden road to Samarkand. Courtesy, of course, of Kosygin and Breshnev, Intourist and Aeroflot, but primarily because a great teacher long ago made it an indispensable part of my life.

＊

A DELAYED-ACTION
TIME BOMB

Harry Cohen

❋✱❋✱❋✱❋✱❋✱❋✱❋✱❋✱❋✱❋✱❋✱❋✱❋✱❋✱

The author and beneficiary of the teaching explosion he describes is Harry Cohen, a practicing attorney and editor of The Advocate, *official publication of the Bronx County Bar Association in New York, of which he is past President. He serves on the Coordinating Committee of the New York City Bar Associations and has been a frequent contributor also to numerous Anglo-Jewish publications.*

❋✱❋✱❋✱❋✱❋✱❋✱❋✱❋✱❋✱❋✱❋✱❋✱❋✱❋✱

＊

A DELAYED-ACTION
TIME BOMB

Harry Cohen

I fled him down labyrinthine ways and down the nights
and days of my torment. I look back and I think of him
as my favorite teacher.

His name was Thaddeus Davis Kenneson, and I sat in
his class for two years in the early 1920's. He had been a
Professor of Law for time out of mind at New York
University's Law School at its Washington Square
"campus" during and following a highly creditable
career at the Bar. He was well in his 60's by then, and
still retained in large degree the bearing and features
which must indeed have distinguished him in any company of men.

Let me describe first of all the incongruity of the
setting. The Law School (since ennobled by endow-
ments) then occupied the upper floor of a building used
in part for factory purposes. The whole area, which was
bounded by a little park, was in the heart of New
York's teeming sweatshops, in one of which, a dozen

years before, 150 employees, chiefly young women, had lost their lives in the famous "Triangle Shirtwaist" fire, still remembered by an older generation of New Yorkers.

Here it was that Professor Kenneson taught his classes, drawn in large measure from the sons of immigrants, many of whom were destined to find places of eminence in the professional, political and business life of the city and nation.

Thaddeus Kenneson had attended Harvard Law School in the golden era which had been ushered in by Dean Langdell, and from which it drew its reputation over many years as America's premier law school—the years during which the school was imperishably linked with the great names of Ames, Thayer, Gray and Beale. Wigmore and Williston were contemporaries of his. To have Professor Kenneson as teacher was to be automatically enrolled in this tradition, transported by his magical evocation of the far away and long ago.

(The names here associated with Professor Kenneson, and which help explain his quality as a teacher of lawyers, represent a group never equaled at any other place or any other time. The whole modern system of teaching law began with Dean Langdell, whose given names were appropriately Christopher Columbus, for he discovered or rather originated the case method which has now been almost universally adopted in this country.

(James Barr Ames, Langdell's successor, an authority on equity jurisprudence and legal history, was one of the first great teachers of the law who never had actually practiced at the Bar. John C. Gray's treatise on future estates and real property became a standard American work. Joseph Beale was the United States authority on conflict of laws, sometimes called "private international law." John H. Wigmore wrote a four-volume treatise on the law of evidence which is not only a work of the ripest scholarship, but perhaps the most frequently quoted text on a legal subject produced in this country. His application of psychological principles to this field long antedate the current vogue. Williston is almost equally outstanding as an authority on the law of contract and sales.

(One can easily see how Kenneson, who had been pupil or contemporary of such men, brought to his teaching in the unpretentious setting of the New York University Law School the best and most hallowed traditions of the American legal system.—*Ed.*)

I said I fled him in fear. How else could it be with a man to whom teaching was a war on ignorance, fought with the vigor of a military campaign? How else could it be with a man who was profoundly convinced that you were abysmally uninstructed? It was only then, when self-abasement was complete, that instruction began. When it did, however, it was marked by a ripeness of scholarship and lucidity of reasoning, the counterpart of which I have not observed. He stood out even in a faculty which included Arthur Vanderbilt, Dean Frank H. Sommer—and Judge Crater, destined soon to take the longest adjournment in legal history.

Professor Kenneson taught me Equity Jurisdiction and Evidence, using (what else?) the casebooks of Ames and Thayer. (He had, himself, done the volume on "Trusts" in the *American Casebook Series.*) For a student not to have read every one of the copious notes in these volumes was, if called upon, to stand in the direst peril; after forty years, I can still hear the explosive force in the first syllable of "*ignorant*" as the word fell from his lips. Not to know, for instance, that Baron Parke was a great judge and Mr. Justice Park a fool (as you can see in your Boswell's *Johnson*) presented no less a hazard. The exposition which followed, however, would lead you to wonder whether "Kenny" had not had a previous incarnation in the days when equity jurisprudence was being fashioned in the English courts.

He was in some measure embittered, I think, and gave evidence of this. To a particularly inane response of a student, he could pause for a withering glance.

"I haven't the slightest doubt," he drawled, "that in time you will be a Supreme Court Judge."

Nor have I yet forgotten the day I had the misfortune to refer to the Corporation of Birmingham (England) as "they" in place of "it," as its corporate status demanded. I was not even offered the comforting assurance of a place on the bench.

Despite the seeming severity, his face could light up with a glint of wintry sunshine at a student's divination or precocity. There was tenderness beneath, and students did not hesitate to ply him with questions between sessions. For this he had endless patience which stemmed from his singular dedication. However, I was not myself among the lucky ones who pursued him between classes. I am sure his influence on others was great, although one would have to make a wide canvas to really know. This much I do know: His name is familiar to more than one generation of lawyers who passed through his hands. No one who had "Kenny" could possibly forget him.

I was among the last of his students. He had suffered a stroke during the preceding summer, and his last class was taught from a wheelchair. I cannot recall that he missed a session. By term's end, Professor Kenneson had passed away.

He earns an honored place in my thoughts by the breadth of his interest in the law, which encompassed the fruits of reason and experience in equal measure. What if, in the nature of things, one could only come to appreciate his worth after one had left his tutelage? Even his method seems to me needed for a profession in which one requires special preparation for the rigors of combat.

Did I love him, my favorite teacher? Not until it was far too late to thank him—not until I came to see that he had carried a time-bomb intended for delayed-action. What I would not give, however, to sit once again at his feet.

✳

"IF YOU
CAN'T EXPRESS IT,
YOU DON'T KNOW IT"

Marya Mannes

*Born into two of music's First Families,
Marya Mannes turned to writing and has
produced distinguished fiction, essays,
poetry and light verse. But perhaps her
criticisms have stirred more readers, especially when her target is broadcasting.
She has appeared on both TV screens and
lecture platforms, was formerly an editor
of* Vogue *and* Glamour *and a staff writer
for* The Reporter.

✳

"IF YOU CAN'T EXPRESS IT, YOU DON'T KNOW IT"*

Marya Mannes

She wore guimpes with boned net collars, gray hair tucked into a nest by combs and pins, and pince-nez on a long filigree chain with a sliding catch. Her name was Miss Sweet and she taught us English composition for six years in a west-side school for young ladies.

Miss Sweet, belying her name, was a tough one.

"Agnes," she would ask of a girl with long mustard curls and a bad skin, "What do you think Keats meant by 'the still unravished bride of quietness'?"

Agnes, who was voluble enough in the locker room and given to hot whispers, laughed nervously.

"Well, I know what he means but I can't express it," she said.

"If you know it," snapped Miss Sweet, "you can express it."

If Miss Sweet had said nothing else during those six

* First published in the *World Journal Tribune's* "Book Week," Dec. 8, 1963, and reprinted by permission of the author and publisher.

years, I would still owe her what I know of writing. She held that clear statement was the result of clear thinking and that sloppy thinking could produce only sloppy writing. She had nothing but scorn for the vague generalities, flowery prose, and loose structure of which most of us were guilty much of the time. And she had ample opportunity to flay us for them since we had to write at least two compositions of three or four hundred words a week for thirty-two weeks a year. Beyond concern for the rules of grammar and proper spelling, these were marked for logic, style and interest.

"Do you know why this was boring?" she would ask, holding up an evening's agonized homework. Silence from the perpetrator, who looked down at her desk.

"It's boring because it bored you. Didn't it?"

"I guess so, Miss Sweet . . . I was tired and . . ."

"Please remember this, girls. What bores you will bore others. Now I am not saying that what delights you is bound to delight others. I have seen enough effusions to realize that enthusiasm is not enough. But, in the reins of discipline, it helps. In contrast, the result of grudging effort is bound to be tedious."

I was one of the effusive kind. Thoroughly awash in romantic literature I would, as narrator, pretend to be Sir Gawain and write a diary of a day at the Round Table and, on another occasion, describe my misery as a serf on a feudal farm. I must say that Miss Sweet permitted amusement to flicker in her small gray eyes as she followed my adventures in time and place, and once she said, "Well, at least you are capable of empathy." (She explained empathy, of course.) The only piece that really seemed to alarm her was something entitled, "The

Call of the Blood." Having spent most of my youth in
an opera box hearing my uncle conduct the Ring cycle,
I drowned in dark Teutonic legends. Drawing heavily
on my Junker blood, although it contributed only a
fourth of my stream, I imagined myself with wings on
my helmet and shining breastplates making horn-hatted
heroes happy in Valhalla. There were gory details on
the way, but what really disturbed Miss Sweet, I think,
were not my Valkyrie rides so much as my tender
ministrations to Siegfried. That is, my imagined Siegfried. She did not realize that all this was an attempt to
blot out the fleshy tenors with bad wigs and bearskins
bobbing on their swelling paunches.

"I wouldn't have thought you quite so primitive," she
said, giving me a B-minus. "Don't you know these were
a brutal lot of people?"

I realized it fifteen years later. But then I was hurt.

Once she said, "I don't for a minute want to curb
your fertile imagination, my child, but why not write
sometime of what you actually see and know?"

"You mean," said I, with worldly sarcasm, "How I
Spent My Vacation?"

"I do not," said Miss Sweet, "but you have an interesting family and an interesting background, and perhaps others would like to hear about it."

"I can't write about Amsterdam Avenue," I said. "It's
so ugly."

She flashed me a look of scorn and walked away.

Miss Sweet was very calm with her speech but very
nervous with her little hands. They were either tucking
a wisp of hair in place or, more often, moving the slide-
ring on her spectacle chain up and down, up and down.

Whether she was silent or not, seated or walking, they had to be busy.

One day we found a goldfish on the top of the classroom bowl, belly up on the water. What to do with it? Miss Sweet was due in five minutes and hated messes. So one of us scooped it up with an exaggerated grimace of loathing, and another said, "Bury it! In the window box!" This we did, with dispatch.

Twenty minutes later Miss Sweet was walking back and forth before us explaining, with passion and reference, why Jane Austen was so good. Every time she got near the window we held our breath, because her hands sometimes left her chain to toy with the plants. But each time she would move away again, sliding her catch up and down.

It was bound, of course, to happen. Giving us a specific assignment on *Pride and Prejudice*, her fingers scrabbled in the dirt of the window and brought up the goldfish. With a strangled "Aagh," she hurled it on the floor and turned on us.

"If this is a joke," she said, her voice cold and shaking, "it is an abominable one." We tried, all at once, to explain; but Miss Sweet left the classroom ten minutes before the end of the period.

Aggrieved in our innocence, we could not understand the root of her violence. Now I believe that, because she was facing it, she hated death.

But Miss Sweet need not have worried, because she is immortal; as all teachers who have implanted visions of worth and beauty in their pupils are immortal.

With love and gratitude, I salute her now.

※

MEMOIR ABOUT AN ECCENTRIC

Brooks Atkinson

✺✺✺✺✺✺✺✺✺✺✺✺✺✺✺✺✺✺✺✺✺✺✺✺✺✺✺✺

Brooks Atkinson, drama critic, foreign correspondent and author, is in a sense a monument to the man of whom he writes here. After three years as editor of "The Book Review" section of The New York Times, *he became its drama critic in 1925 and, with the exception of the war years, served in that capacity and as critic at large until 1965.*

✺✺✺✺✺✺✺✺✺✺✺✺✺✺✺✺✺✺✺✺✺✺✺✺✺✺✺✺

MEMOIR
ABOUT AN
ECCENTRIC

Brooks Atkinson

Among the gift books I have cherished for years is a Collegiate Edition of *Webster's Dictionary*. The flyleaf inscription is: "For Brooks Atkinson, with the kind regards of C. T. Copeland. 23 Dec. 1916." The word "underhanded" appears at the bottom of the page.

Charles Townsend Copeland was a valiant teacher of English literature and composition at Harvard. To save himself the drudgery of reading what his students composed, he required them to appear at his room on the top floor of Hollis Hall and read their themes aloud. While the student droned on in a frightened voice, Copey (as everyone called him) slumped in a chair by the fireplace, emitting groans and generally indicating agony and despair.

On December 23, 1916 (why wasn't I home on recess?) I had used the word "underhanded" in some forgotten example of prose.

"There is no such word," Copey exclaimed. "The

word is 'underhand.' " I remember demurring. "If you can find 'underhanded' in the dictionary, I'll give it to you," he retorted.

In the text of the dictionary the word "underhanded" is marked with a jaunty arrow in Copey's hand. He accepted defeat handsomely.

Copey made an indelible impression on everyone who studied with him. With good reason, we were known as "Copey's disciples." As years went on he became the idol of a cult. There were many finer scholars on the Harvard faculty. There were nobler spirits. But Copey was unique because he was an effective teacher who was also an eccentric person.

Since I have been writing professionally for almost a half century after having performed my duties as a college student, I cannot pretend that I consciously follow his instructions today. But Copey's petulant criticism of empty rhetoric permanently scarred my soul. The dangling participle (everyone dangles a participle sooner or later) is something I equate with moral shame. Copey hated monotonous sentence structure. "Good old subject, good old predicate," he used to say bitterly. He highly approved of the periodic sentence that makes a reader go on to the end.

He insisted on a visible transition from one paragraph to the next. No doubt he had crotchets, but I don't remember any in the sphere of English composition. I have never questioned the principles that he reiterated as he squirmed with impatience and disgust in his chair.

Copey was also an actor. As students, we probably did not use that word to describe his personality. But his style was histrionic. He was a short man with a large head. He wore large, round, metal-rimmed glasses—one pair for general use, another for reading. The measured dignity with which he changed one pair for the other was excellent theater. It put his audience in an expectant frame of mind.

He was childishly vain. In my senior year I was his secretary: wrote his letters, deposited and cashed his checks, bought his straw hat for the summer, rummaged through his private papers in his bank vault when he was looking for something. I even computed the grades for his students according to a mathematical system that was fool-proof, although of course he reviewed the grades before he filed them with the dean.

During this year of happy servitude I was frequently mortified by the size and nature of his vanity. A year or two later, he angrily denounced me on the street because he thought I had not done him full justice in a familiar essay I had written for *Scribner's Magazine*. After that wounding episode we had no communication for several years.

Then he was mollified by an appreciative remark I made about him in an article on Harvard College in the *Harvard Alumni Bulletin*. It was soothing to be on good terms with him again. But the original cordiality could never be recovered. I felt that I had been badly treated by a man I had served and venerated. I still venerate him as a teacher. He taught me that good writing is both difficult and honorable.

＊

A TIP
OF THE HAT
TO MR. B.

Malcolm A. Hoffmann

A specialist in the antitrust laws who made the O. Henry Roll of Honor with his first short story, Fraternity, *lawyer-author Malcolm A. Hoffmann has created a highly successful practice at the bar and published fiction, book reviews, legal articles and books such as* Government Lawyer *for laymen and* Antitrust Laws and Techniques *for the professional. With the editor of this book, he puts out an occasional publication of comment called* Back and Forth.

✳

A TIP
OF THE HAT
TO MR. B.

Malcolm A. Hoffmann

I have come to that age where I ache to find out where I have been; the past has become important—the old joys sometimes glimmer at night, the old pains sometimes throb. From the infinity of memories there lob up good and bad appositions, men and women, the books I have read, and the thousand details of days and nights. But let the mind seek out its influences, and it is the teachers, formal and informal, who stand out.

The school teachers now seem gigantic in their authority, their claims to knowledge, and their eagerness to share it with me. They included the fact men and women: those who went their routine ways trying to project the Latin conjugations, the date and participants in the Treaty of Vienna and the axioms of Euclid. These were the ambient encyclopedias, and the day-laborers of knowledge; most of my teachers are to be counted among them, and, of course, I needed them as much as the police and fire departments, the highways, and other public services. Much that they taught me has long been forgotten. But there were a few others, and I was fortunate in viewing a scholarly heaven in which there were pulsating new, bright stars. The names remain clear, the faces, the mannerisms, even some of the words. These were giants holding attitudes of mind valid for an age in which truth was unattainable, but the search as necessary as food or breath.

I shall ignore the lawmen, the great professors skilled in the ambush of fact and concept: Thomas Read Powell, Felix Frankfurter, Warren Abner Seavey, Zechariah Chafee and many others. My mind was already shaped for good or evil by the time I studied law. There were the college giants: George Lyman Kittredge, Alfred North Whitehead, John Livingston Lowes, Roger Bigelow Merriman, Bernard De Voto— this was a treasure trove of able men, and all shaped and turned my mind like a piece of soft clay.

But behind them loom the real giants, the ones who first showed that the written word was not sacred and that all the millions of words on which the eyes would falter in a lifetime are no more significant than the droppings of pigeons unless they are appraised by a roving and critical brain. They were the first with their cajolery, their wiles, their ruses to implant learning in unenthusiastic young minds. They had the advantage of writing on clean blackboards, of talking first at a time when words would be remembered best, of putting down a mark which would sear itself into the soul.

He bore the improbable name of Armona C. Beverly, and taught history at White Plains High School in suburban New York. This was not a school that had made a reputation for training scholars. If it has fathered any great intellects, we have not been told about them. In 1930 it did send its fair share of graduates to the big universities and they thrived well. It sent to the world automobile mechanics, violinists, college professors, satisfying our middle-class destinies as well as other high schools. But I wander from the image of Mr. Beverly.

In 1929 New Rochelle, White Plains' traditional rival, defeated White Plains in football, 45–0. In that year White Plains hired as coach a professional football player who was paid more than the principal. When the appointment leaked out I wrote an editorial against it in the school paper, *The Orange,* but this was not a powerful voice, and for many years thereafter White Plains enjoyed the doubtful distinction of being invincible in Westchester football. Mr. Beverly anticipated and disliked this eventuality, its inappropriateness in a society which already had learned to place too much value upon the unreal and the self-defeating. Beverly referred us to a book by John L. Tunis, a *New York Times* sportswriter—the title has escaped me—which piteously exposed professionalism in collegiate sports. He was with the angels on this and almost every issue, a position which almost always is the minority since, as everyone knows, Hell is more heavily populated than Heaven.

He stood in front of the classroom—large, well-cleaned windows to the left, the corridor door on the right, forty scholars in between, old lithographs of Washington and Lincoln on the wall; I remember that the windows were to my left because "Doll" H— sat next to one and when the sun was strong and her dress thin it was difficult to concentrate on either American or Modern European History. Mr. Beverly had a square Mt. Rushmore-like face, and drily spoke his skepticism to an audience opening its mind between two wars, at the eve of depression, but an audience which still held fast to eternal verities: the charm of Greta Garbo, the adventure of a Sabbatini novel, and the concept that even the meanest among us might one day be President.

At another level of life this was the era of pacifism and the muckraker. Mr. Beverly burned with a horror of phoniness. If Hayes' *Modern European History* reported that when the Germans went through Belgium in World War I the soldiers committed grim atrocities, including the amputation of nurses' breasts, Mr. Beverly had us read Lord Ponsonby's *War Lies*. As I remember it now, Ponsonby was in charge of World War I British propaganda and later claimed authorship of most of the atrocity stories. When the papers reveled in the veniality of Jimmie Walker, Mr. Beverly felt no surprise. He recommended Lincoln Steffens' *The Shame of the Cities* to the point that corruption was the expectable norm in the management of big cities. The presence of our marines in Nicaragua caused Mr. Beverly to assign Scott Nearing's *Dollar Diplomacy*. That was pretty stiff going in our little Republican town. I have not seen the book since, but I remember it saddened us with its talk of American imperialism in Latin America; we were proud of Wilson and what he called the "New Freedom," but Muzzey's *History of the American People* taught us that we had imposed a Pax American upon Latin America. We believed in our freedom, and we thought that there must be moral content in public matters, particularly in the movement of our troops.

Mr. Beverly led us little by little to a point of view that was ready to question anything, and regarded nothing as a "sacred cow."

Mr. Beverly stood in front of the room, a firm pillar of righteousness, challenging the falsehoods of man, both public and private. His heroes were Jefferson, Lincoln and Theodore Roosevelt. He asked whether the United States had ever waged an aggressive war, a challenging question to the dewy-eyed innocents of 1930. To the outraged negative he replied with a description of President Lincoln's "Spot Resolutions." Lincoln in Congress had challenged the statement of President Polk that Mexico had started the war by first spilling American blood on American soil. "Show us the spot," the indignant Lincoln had cried out, and so more than ninety years later did Mr. Beverly, as we all cringed in our chairs feeling the collective guilt of the Mexican War.

This heresy proved a little too much for the staid editor of *The White Plains Daily Reporter*, the local molder of public opinion, which was willing to enter political controversy provided it was a century old. It doubted whether Mr. Beverly was suited for his teaching position, and suggested that the local Superintendent of Schools conduct an inquiry. We had learned too much to let the matter alone. A number of us traipsed down to the Superintendent's office and were among the angels speaking for Mr. B., who was vindicated on more important grounds than our testimony.

I remember writing a good, sound, sixteen-year-old's letter to the "Open Forum" column of *The Reporter*, which was first acknowledged by an editorial explaining why the paper would not engage in editorial debate with a high school boy, and then said that if I would identify myself the letter would be printed. Over the vault of years I remember well that it was printed with a typographical error in almost every line.

I do not hesitate any longer to say that I was one of Mr. B.'s favorites. It comes to me now that I sat near the front, and one morning was contemplating historical verities while munching on a Milky Way, badly hidden behind my spiral notebook. "Hoffmann" bellowed Mr. B., "this is not the cafeteria. Leave the room at once and don't return until you have finished eating." And then, with a great show of anger, he followed me down the aisle and out the door into the corridor. "Give me half," he said, "I'm starving."

I have read great books and known great teachers. My mind has lumbered through a large and important period of American history that has swirled on with me on this uncertain planet. I do not pretend to have understood most of what has happened since I left White Plains High, but I have accepted little that was precooked for me and thought more about the bases of my faith because of Mr. Beverly. When he gave us Mencken he gave us a scalpel and not a bomb. He did not leave us in despair but in confidence that free inquiry is a national asset. He loved our egalitarian national dream, but made us familiar with Goldsmith's happy phrase, "a citizen of the world." More than anything else we learned to partake of skeptical, pragmatic inquiry, in my view America's most lasting contribution to this generation's civilization. We were bathed in freedom's dream, and held that nothing was unobtainable to a searching mind in this land where the Indian trails climb over huge snow-capped mountains, and the prairie lands sweep their rich fields farther than you and I can travel in three days in a Model A Ford.

Mr. Beverly, to you I tip the derby hat we seniors wore in 1930.

☀

FIFTH GRADE
IN
ST. LOUIS

David Loth

✳

FIFTH GRADE
IN
ST. LOUIS

David Loth

Long before I realized how much she had done for me, I had completely forgotten her name. Even her face is a blur in memory, a lovely pale blur topped by a lot of red hair. Her voice is clearer, rather high and sharp with an accent then strange to Midwestern ears—she came from such a far eastern place as Indiana. Her job was to teach grammar, literature, arithmetic, history and art to twenty-five or thirty children of the fifth grade in St. Louis's Eugene Field School. She taught me to meet and get to know other people without suffering agonies of self-consciousness and doubt.

As I look back at our relationship, I can see that she took extra pains with me. I think she did it because our introduction to each other was a thoroughly uncomfortable experience for both of us. Through no real fault of either, we shared a few moments of acute embarrassment, and they brought out all the sympathy in her nature, an unusually altruistic and perceptive one.

I was nine years old and spending my first day in a regular school. Up to this time my mother, who before her marriage had been a teacher of retarded children and now lectured on literary and philosophical topics at women's clubs, had given me lessons at home. She had considered me backward, although years later she acknowledged that probably I seemed so only in comparison to my elder brother and sister, prodigies of learning before they were five, as I was frequently informed. On the whole, however, she had been very nice about my shortcomings, tutoring me gently and kindly but diligently. Now she had decided I was fit to take my place in a class with my contemporaries, and marched me off to Eugene Field.

Timing was not one of her strong points, so she had waited until the new term was about two weeks old to enroll me in the grade she thought I should grace. At the very beginning I might have been less noticeable, sharing the spotlight with a transfer student or two and the new teacher.

While Mother's instruction had qualified me more than adequately in an academic sense, I was woefully unprepared socially. I was by nature as shy as a boy can be, and had been indulged in my shyness. I had never met more than one other child at a time, and seldom played with more than one except at an occasional birthday party. If I refused an invitation from the boy next door to join a baseball game on the corner lot because I preferred to read a book at home, my choice was approved as a laudable desire to improve my mind. It did not occur to the gregarious members of the family that I secluded myself not because I loved learning but because I was afraid of people.

Here in this fifth grade classroom were more kids than I'd ever seen in one place before, and all of them were complete strangers to me. They were all staring at me, too, the blank but not hostile, not friendly stare of the pack contemplating an outsider who may either be accepted or devoured. As the redheaded teacher introduced me to them, it seemed pretty plain to me that I would be devoured. But I was too scared to run. Meekly I crept to the desk which she indicated near the side wall.

Mercifully she informed me that my first assignment would be to work by myself on some arithmetic problems—she wanted to see if I really was up to the standards of the class. As soon as she supplied me with the necessary tools—a nice sharp pencil, a large sheet of white foolscap and a half sheet torn from a yellow scratch pad—I knew I was in serious difficulty.

One of my mother's foibles was a miserly attitude toward any store-bought paper. No one wrote upon a virgin page in our house except for the most formal correspondence or a manuscript to be sent to an editor. For my lessons we made do with whatever scraps were at hand—old envelopes, the backs of memos or circulars, the blank lower half of a letter. But my eyesight would be conserved, Mother thought, if the scrap rested upon a clean white background, so I was allowed one sheet for this purpose, strictly for show, never for use.

Naturally I supposed that this was the common practice, and at my new desk I rested the small yellow scrap on the larger white one and bent to my task.

The problems were long division, I recall. There simply was not enough room on the scratch paper to work them out, only for the answers. It never occurred to me that I was permitted the luxury of space for tentative, private scribblings. I assumed that I was meant to solve the problems in my head, a remarkably tough challenge, but I tried and set down only the answers as I figured them. When Teacher saw what I was doing, she told me to stay a few moments at recess and she would explain how work was done. Meanwhile, she asked with obvious doubt in her tone, did I know how to diagram a sentence? I did.

"Very well," she said, "write this down and diagram it on the blackboard while we go on with the lesson."

She dictated, and as I scribbled hastily on another bit of yellow paper I was profoundly shocked. What I understood her to say in her crisp, clear Eastern accent was:

"Man wants but little hair below nor wants that little long."

Later when I told Mother about the astonishing choice of language by school teachers, she was inclined to blame me for being so unfamiliar with the works of Oliver Goldsmith that I did not know the key word was "here" not "hair." (She was fair enough to admit after her initial disappointment in me that maybe she was at fault for permitting such a heinous gap in my early reading.)

Meanwhile, in class, I went obediently but unhappily

to the blackboard. The proper procedure, as I knew, was to compose the diagram and then inscribe the sentence neatly below. When I wrote this out the laughter began, cruel, frightening laughter. Teacher turned, frowning, and the frown froze on her face while her clear white skin flushed a deeper pink even than my burning cheeks. With quick presence of mind she seized an eraser and rubbed out my work, saying:

"Very good, that was very good."

"But how could she have told so fast whether I'd diagrammed it right or not?" I asked Mother that night when she inquired how my day had gone.

Teacher recovered from her embarrassment a lot faster than I did, I think, and I never would have been able to recover at all but for her. She must have wanted to get out of that room for a moment at least to compose herself. Perhaps she saw that I was even more miserable than she. I'd looked only once at those grinning, smirking faces and now was gazing fixedly at my toes. Gently Teacher put a hand on my shoulder and guided me back to my seat.

I remained there, huddled in my shame, yet not knowing exactly what I was ashamed of, until recess. Dimly I heard her ordering the class to open some book or other to some page or other. I paid no attention to them, nor did she to me. At the recess the class trooped out, but I lingered uncertainly by my desk. Teacher, too, had started for the door, then turned back. She informed me that I was doing quite well for a first day—I wonder if she ever asked God to forgive her the little white lie—and that I might now join the other children in the yard or the basement.

"Do I have to?" I asked.

"No, but they'll think it peculiar if you don't," was her reply. "We'll talk about your arithmetic tomorrow."

Reluctantly I dragged myself outdoors and stood against a wall for what seemed hours. No one paid the slightest heed to me, but I had the sensation of crowds pointing and snickering. At one point I saw Teacher in the doorway across a sea of terrifying, running, shouting people. She smiled at me and was gone.

I don't remember much about the rest of the day except that I didn't eat the lunch Mother had packed for me, a lapse which was a full measure of my misery. Not a single child spoke to me, either, and I guess I was grateful for their forbearance. She noticed, and in the days that followed she created for me various opportunities to get acquainted with them and to build my own self-confidence. She did it so unostentatiously that I realized only years later what had happened to me. She could easily have pushed me forward as a teacher's pet, and destroyed me in the process, but she was much too wise for that.

After that first dreadful day she was careful to ask me how I had been taught to do things before she called on me to do them. She found out that I could read aloud fairly well and with more assurance than I usually displayed, so she always called on me just after someone who read very badly had sat down.

She kept me after school quite often because of petty offenses for which no other member of the class was penalized—I think she invented "squirming" as a misdemeanor for me alone. At least I don't remember anyone else being even accused of it, much less punished for it. But when she did order me to stay, she always had one or two others there, detained for some real crime such as throwing spitballs or pinching girls.

She forced us to spend the disciplinary hour in improving conversation, and drew me easily enough into it. She would start us off by reading something, a short poem or a passage from a play or an historical anecdote, and insist that we tell each other what it meant to us and why. That was hard work, and by the time we escaped from this dreadful ordeal of using our minds, we had achieved the solid camaraderie of felons after a prison break. In a matter of weeks I became buddy-buddy with the most unruly and therefore the most highly respected kids in the class.

In a dozen other ways, Teacher saw to it unobtrusively that I played or studied with my peers, so that gradually I lost my fear of them.

I don't remember that I learned anything else at all that term. On the other hand, I don't remember that I ever again learned anything so important. It was my good luck that I had been well tutored in the arithmetic, grammar and history to which my new companions were being subjected, so I was in effect repeating the fifth grade, although I was careful not to say so at home or at school. I never had it so easy in any other phase of my formal education, and because I didn't have to waste much time on lessons, I could concentrate on studying my classmates. With Teacher's help I learned how to talk with them, and listen too.

The public schools of that time and place contained a fair cross section of the white population of the city. At

Eugene Field we had the offspring of the wealthiest mercantile family in town as well as a few patched and darned progeny of those on the ragged edge of privation. Private schools were maintained exclusively, as far as we heard, for kids who were too stupid to win promotion on their merits and whose parents could afford to spare them the humiliation of being "kept back." In the early grades a variety of foreign accents were encountered, especially German because even in many second generation St. Louis families the tongue of the Fatherland was still spoken. However, by the fifth grade, most of these children had learned to speak comprehensible English.

Those were the years when the automobile was beginning to replace the horse and buggy but was far from having done it. High status still attached to the horseshoer's boy and the liveryman's son. Among my comrades in those penalty sessions after school was a tough, cocky ten-year-old whose father was head groom at the stables of one of the great mansions near the park. Bud had been known to chew tobacco, and was the recognized leader of the fifth grade in all extracurricular activities.

Across the street from the school was a vast empty lot nearly half a square block. It served us as an auxiliary playground and in winter was the scene of tremendous, organized snowball fights. We constructed elaborate snow forts and ramparts, and Bud was always captain of our grade in these combats. The highest honor of my elementary school career came the day he promoted me to lieutenant on the field of battle.

My education progressed so fast that by the time

spring arrived I wasn't afraid to meet new people in or out of school. My shyness was replaced by what I have since heard called brashness.

Before the school year was ended we moved to Chicago, and thanks to that redheaded teacher I survived and even thrived on the change. St. Louis, when I lived there, was as thoroughly segregated as any Southern city; in fact, it prided itself on being a Southern city. Chicago's public schools actually enrolled Negro kids along with the whites. Her training enabled me to adjust to them and to the new strange environment in a couple of weeks.

She had done so well by me that I took her great gift for granted and promptly forgot all about her. I don't suppose that I thought of her once until a day fourteen years later when I was on the staff of the old *New York World*, and its spectacular executive editor, Herbert Bayard Swope, was conferring upon me the accolade of his approval. He had his own special high-handed way of doing it, and I was not yet accustomed to it or him. He had been born with a royal manner and cultivated it to the hilt. He knew also that sugar tastes sweeter if swallowed right after something bitter. He had called me in to tell me I was to be cable editor, a dizzy promotion for a twenty-three-year-old, but he led up to the announcement by barking at me:

"You know, the trouble with you is you have too much ego in your cosmos."

Well, he should have been able to tell. There never was a better expert on the human ego than HBS. His own was as big as a man can have and remain at large in the community—three or four times life size. He thought he was deflating mine, I'm sure, and yet I wasn't shaking with fear. In fact, I found myself perversely taking his remark as a compliment. At the same time, I wondered why I wasn't scared in the presence of this irresistible, primitive natural force; most of the younger members of *The World's* staff were intimidated by him. All of a sudden I remembered Teacher— was it because she and Swope were both redheaded? Thanks to her I could stand in the presence of the Swopes of this world and not be tongue-tied or ill at ease. She had given me a little of the power to see and appraise others, not always be looking inward at myself in fear and discomfort.

She must be in her eighties now, and at last I can do what I never thought of doing then, nor would have dared to do. Across the years I blow a kiss to that young woman who in 1909 was teaching fifth grade at the Eugene Field School in St. Louis.